HARCOURT

Math

Challenge Workbook

TEACHER EDITION
Grade 4

Harcourt

Orlando   Austin   Chicago   New York   Toronto   London   San Diego

Visit The Learning Site!
www.harcourtschool.com

REPRODUCING COPIES FOR STUDENTS

This Teacher's Edition contains full-size student pages
with answers printed in non-reproducible blue ink.

It may be necessary to adjust the exposure control on
your photocopy machine to a lighter setting to ensure
that blue answers do not reproduce.

ISBN 0-15-336518-8

5 6 7 8 9 10 054 10 09 08 07 06 05

CONTENTS

Broken Records

Read each world record for the largest collection. Write the
missing digit. Then write the letter above the digit at the bottom
of the page to answer the question.

1. Pencils: five thousand, five hundred ___5__,500 (W)

2. Pig-related items: two thousand, two hundred fifty 2,__2__50 (A)

3. Movie cameras: four hundred forty 4__4__0 (G)

4. Refrigerator magnets: twenty-nine thousand 2__9__,000 (S)

5. Bunny-related items: eight thousand, four hundred
   thirty-seven 8,4__3__7 (M)

6. Four-leaf clovers: seventy-two thousand,
   nine hundred twenty-eight __7__2,928 (R)

7. Banana-related items: seventeen thousand __1__7,000 (U)

8. Badges: eight thousand, six hundred sixty-two __8__,662 (P)

9. Televisions and radios: ten thousand, sixty 10,0__6__0 (E)

10. Frog-related items: one thousand, two hundred two 1,2__0__2 (B)

11. What does John collect?

   B   U   B   B   **L**   E   G   U   M
   _0_ _1_ _0_ _0_   _6_ _4_ _1_ _3_

   W   R   A   P   P   E   R   S
   _5_ _7_ _2_ _8_ _8_ _6_ _7_ _9_

Spin That Number

Work Together

Use a pencil and a paper clip to make a spinner like the one shown.

Play this game with a partner. Each player spins the paper clip six times. The player's score is the number that the paper clip points to. The other player keeps score, using tally marks.

After each round, find the total value for each player. The player with the higher value wins. Play three rounds. Totals will vary.

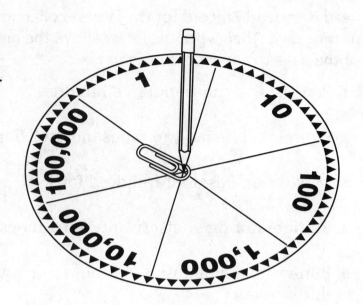

Sample Scorecard

Name	100,000	10,000	1,000	100	10	1	Total Value
Lu		/	//	//		/	12,201
Miguel	//		/	/	/	/	201,111 winner

1.
Scorecard

Name	100,000	10,000	1,000	100	10	1	Total Value

2.

3.

4. What is the highest possible total value for one round? ___600,000___

Name _____

Sun to Planet

Planet	Approximate Distance from the Sun (in Miles)
Mercury	36,000,000
Venus	67,000,000
Earth	93,000,000
Mars	141,000,000
Jupiter	486,000,000
Saturn	892,000,000

1. Which two planets are closest together?

   Venus and Earth

2. Which planet is about twice as far from the sun as Mercury is?

   Venus

3. What is the distance between Earth and Saturn?

   about 799,000,000 mi

4. Which planet is closest to Earth?

   Venus

5. Which planet is closest to Jupiter?

   Mars

6. Which two planets are about 856,000,000 miles apart?

   Mercury and Saturn

7. Which planet is about ten times as far from the sun as Earth is?

   Saturn

Just Down the Road a Bit

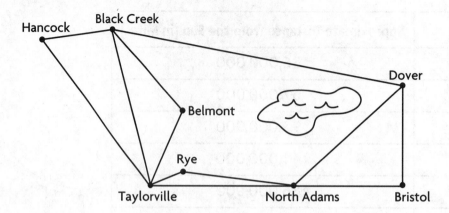

The distance from Taylorville to Rye is 10 miles.

Use the map. Estimate the distances. Accept answers close to estimates given.

1. Taylorville to North Adams _about 40 miles_

2. Hancock to Black Creek _about 20 miles_

3. Bristol to Dover _about 25 miles_

4. Belmont to Black Creek _about 30 miles_

5. Taylorville to Hancock _about 50 miles_

6. The distance between Taylorville and North Adams is about the same as the distance between which other two towns?

   Taylorville and Black Creek, or North Adams and Dover

7. The distance between which two towns is about 2 times as great as the distance between Rye and Taylorville?

   Hancock and Black Creek, or Taylorville and Belmont

8. It takes Don longer to bicycle from Bristol to North Adams than to bicycle from Bristol to Dover, although the distance is shorter. Explain why this might be so.

   Possible answer: The terrain is hillier between Bristol

   and North Adams than between Bristol and Dover.

CW4 Challenge

Name _____

The Complete Picture

Complete the pictograph and the chart using the information provided.

The Five Most Populated States in the USA and their Estimated Populations

California: 35,000,000

Florida: _____15,000,000_____

Illinois: 10,000,000

New York: 20,000,000

Texas: _____20,000,000_____

The Five Most Populated States in the U.S.A.	
California	☺ ☺ ☺ ☾
Florida	☺ ☾
Illinois	☺
New York	☺ ☺
Texas	☺ ☺
Key: Each ☺ = _10 million_ people.	

1. Explain how you completed your chart and pictograph.

_____Answers will vary._____

_____

_____

_____

2. Could the sixth most populated state have an estimated population of fourteen million? Explain.

_____No, its population would have to be less than_____

_____that of Illinois._____

Estimate the Point

You can estimate the position of a point on a number line.
Use the number line to estimate the position of 42.

Think: 42 is between 40 and 50.

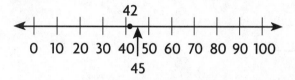

Step 1: 45 is halfway between 40 and 50.
Locate 45 on the number line.

Step 2: 42 is closer to 40 than to 45.
Plot a point to approximate the position of 42.
Label the point 42.

Estimate the position of each point on the number line.
Check students' work.

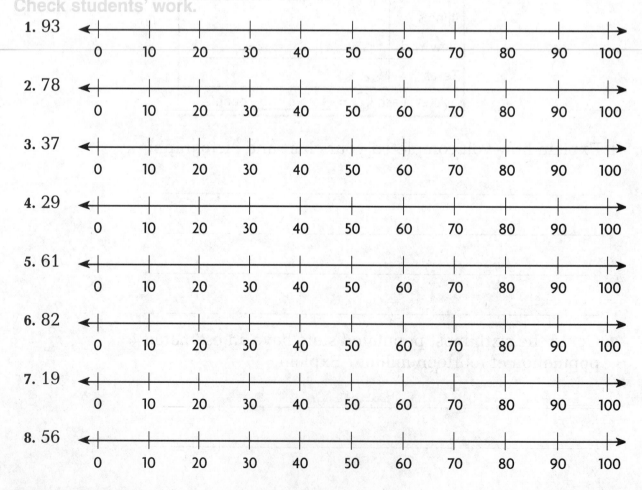

1. 93

2. 78

3. 37

4. 29

5. 61

6. 82

7. 19

8. 56

Name _____

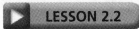

In Between

For 1–8, fill in the blanks by choosing one of the numbers from the box.

1,335	5,160	57	2,015,675
349	498	3,145,000	15,721
5,289	615,460	1,672	4,900
3,456	572	1,020	365
29	3,450,000	43	15,440

1. Heights of mountains in feet: 1,535 > ___1,335___ > 1,025

2. Temperatures in degrees Celsius: 25 < ___29___ < 36

3. Populations of cities: 615,450 < ___615,460___ < 615,490

4. Lengths of tunnels in feet: 5,280 > ___5,160___ > 5,046

5. Ages of trees in years: 241 < ___349___ < 356

6. Lengths of rivers in miles: 3,710 > ___3,456___ > 2,980

7. Numbers of stamps in collections: 490 < ___498___ < 563

8. Numbers of mosquitoes in swamps: 2,500,000 < ___3,145,000___ < 3,300,000

For 9–14, circle the number that is between the greatest number and the least number.

9. Depths of lakes in feet: (328)   230   390

10. Heights of mountains in feet: 20,320   14,573   (14,730)

11. Heights of volcanic eruptions in feet: 9,991   (9,175)   9,003

12. Numbers of Kennel Club collies registered: 14,025   14,281   (14,073)

13. Highest recorded Alaska temperatures: 107   (112)   115

14. Daily log-ons to the internet   3,673,471   (3,841,391)   3,897,100

Miles to Go

Mileage Chart	Charleston, SC	Jacksonville, FL	New Orleans, LA	New York, NY	Raleigh, NC	Tallahassee, FL	Washington, D.C.
Charleston, SC		239	781	764	281	404	525
Jacksonville, FL	239		546	940	455	165	702
New Orleans, LA	781	546		1,324	860	390	1,085
New York, NY	764	940	1,324		492	1,105	238
Raleigh, NC	281	455	860	492		615	256
Tallahassee, FL	404	165	390	1,105	615		868
Washington, D.C.	525	702	1,085	238	256	868	

Follow these steps to find the driving distance between New York, NY, and Tallahassee, FL.

- Locate New York along the top of the chart. Locate Tallahassee along the side of the chart.

- Follow the column down, and the row across.

- The number at which they intersect is the driving distance, in miles, between them.

So, the driving distance between New York and Tallahassee is 1,105 miles.

The Coronado family traveled from New York to Charleston, SC, in 3 days. Use the mileage chart to find the number of miles they traveled each day.

1.

   DAY 1
   New York, NY
   to
   Washington, D.C.
   238 miles

2.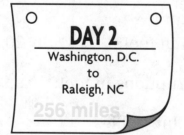

   DAY 2
   Washington, D.C.
   to
   Raleigh, NC
   256 miles

3.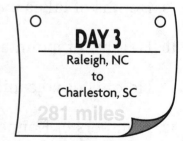

   DAY 3
   Raleigh, NC
   to
   Charleston, SC
   281 miles

4. On which day did they travel the greatest distance? the least distance?

Day 3; Day 1

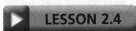

Basketball Bonanza

The basketball club held a contest to guess the number of points famous players scored in their career. Winners got a basketball autographed with the player's name. Guesses closest to the players' scores won. These are the winning guesses.

Billy guessed 27,300.

Shaun guessed 30,000.

Terry guessed 26,500.

Willie guessed 31,400.

Antoine guessed 38,400.

Samantha guessed 26,700.

Pat guessed 27,400.

Jon guessed 26,400.

Place the name of the winner on the basketball.

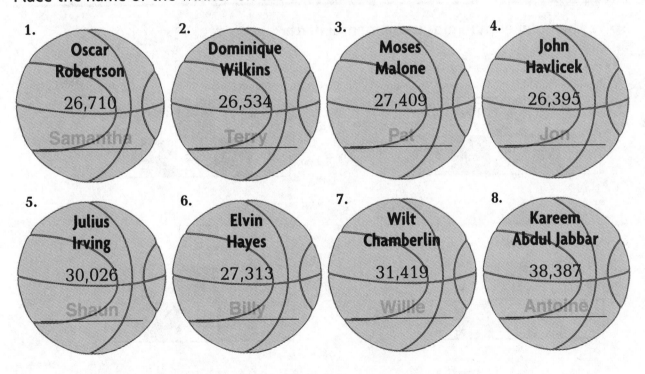

1. Oscar Robertson
26,710
Samantha

2. Dominique Wilkins
26,534
Terry

3. Moses Malone
27,409
Pat

4. John Havlicek
26,395
Jon

5. Julius Irving
30,026
Shaun

6. Elvin Hayes
27,313
Billy

7. Wilt Chamberlin
31,419
Willie

8. Kareem Abdul Jabbar
38,387
Antoine

9. If you round the scores to the nearest thousand, which four players have the same score?

Moses Malone, Elvin Hayes, Oscar Robertson,

and Dominique Wilkins

10. Who scored the most points in his career?

Kareem Abdul Jabbar

Number Pyramids

Number pyramids gain new squares by adding together the two numbers in the squares beneath. Use this simple pattern:

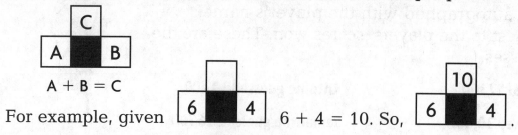

| C |
| A | B |

A + B = C

For example, given | 6 | | 4 | 6 + 4 = 10. So, | 10 | 6 | 4 |.

Depending on which numbers are given, you may also use subtraction: C − B = A or C − A = B.

Solve the number pyramids using mental math.

1.

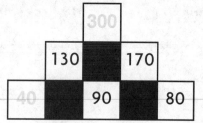

300
130 — 170
40 — 90 — 80

2.

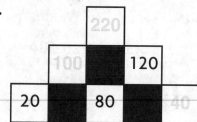

220
100 — 120
20 — 80 — 40

3.

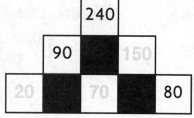

240
90 — 150
20 — 70 — 80

4.

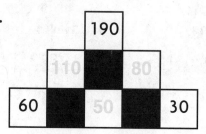

190
110 — 80
60 — 50 — 30

5.

260
150 — 110
80 — 70 — 40

6.

350
180 — 170
80 — 100 — 70

7. Make two of your own pyramids. Check students' work.

Estimating Populations

POPULATIONS: 1790 – 1820				
State	1790	1800	1810	1820
Connecticut	237,655	251,002	261,942	275,248
Massachusetts	378,556	422,845	472,040	523,287
New Hampshire	141,899	183,858	214,460	244,161
Rhode Island	69,112	69,122	76,931	83,059

The table shows how the populations of four New England states changed from 1790–1820. Use the table to answer the questions. Estimate each answer by rounding to the nearest ten thousand and by using front-end estimation.

1. About how many people lived in either New Hampshire or Connecticut in 1790?

   about 380,000 people; about 300,000 people

2. About how many people lived in either Connecticut or Massachusetts in 1820?

   about 800,000 people; about 700,000 people

3. About how many more people lived in Massachusetts than New Hampshire in 1820?

   about 280,000 more people; about 300,000 more people

4. About how many more people lived in New Hampshire in 1820 than in 1790?

   about 100,000 more people; about 100,000 more people

5. About how many people lived in the four New England states in 1790?

   about 830,000 people; about 600,000 people

6. About how many people lived in the four New England states in 1820?

   about 1,120,000 people; about 900,000 people

7. About how many more people lived in the four New England states in 1820 than in 1790?

   about 290,000 more people; about 300,000 more people

Name _____

Money Math

Write each amount from the box below in a money bag to make
the number sentences true.

| $645 | $2,107 | $1,310 | $2,306 |
| $1,632 | $448 | $1,099 | $893 |

1. $1,685 − ($893) = $792

2. ($1,310) + $576 = $1,886

3. $690 + $409 = ($1,099)

4. $2,257 − ($645) = $1,612

5. $923 + $1,184 = ($2,107)

6. ($2,306) − $456 = $1,850

7. $1,945 − ($448) = $1,497

8. ($1,632) + $1,163 = $2,795

9. If you put the money from each money bag into one
large money bag, will you be putting in an amount that
is greater than or less than $10,000?

_____ greater than $10,000

CW12 Challenge

Daily Cross-Number Puzzle

Find the difference. Enter your answers in the cross-number puzzle.

Across

1. 300
− 158
142

4. 284
− 102
182

7. 2,000
− 1,177
823

8. 1,400
− 1,113
287

9. 800
− 685
115

10. 10,000
− 9,925
75

11. 5,001
− 2,438
2,563

14. 1,710
− 189
1,521

15. 10,201
− 2,238
7,963

18. 501
− 402
99

19. 9,007
− 4,789
4,218

20. 324
− 226
98

The cross-number puzzle grid:

1:1	2:4	3:2	■	4:1	5:8	6:2
7:8	2	3	■	8:2	8	7
9:1	1	5	■	7	■	■
10:7	5	■	11:2	5	12:6	13:3
■	■	■	14:1	5	2	1
15:7	16:9	17:6	3	■	18:9	9
19:4	2	1	8	■	20:9	8

Down

1. 3,008
− 1,191
1,817

2. 5,200
− 985
4,215

3. 700
− 465
235

4. 25,000
− 12,245
12,755

5. 1,280
− 1,192
88

6. 1,000
− 973
27

11. 4,003
− 1,865
2,138

12. 10,106
− 3,807
6,299

13. 8,907
− 5,709
3,198

15. 104
− 30
74

16. 9,001
− 8,909
92

17. 3,114
− 3,053
61

Name _____

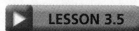

My Balance!

Ted forgot to enter all of his checks and deposits into his check register. Fill in the missing information from these checks to help Ted find the balance in his account.

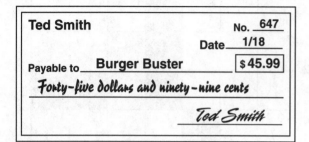

Ted Smith	No. 647
Date	1/18
Payable to Burger Buster	$ 45.99
Forty-five dollars and ninety-nine cents	
	Ted Smith

Ted Smith	No. 650
Date	1/20
Payable to Walkin' Wear	$ 56.00
Fifty-six dollars and no cents	
	Ted Smith

Check Number	Date	Description	Amount of Check	Amount of Deposit	Balance
					$897.54
645	1/17	Shirts Galore	$38.75		$858.79
646	1/18	Newton News	$16.88		$841.91
	1/18	paycheck		$325.76	$1,167.67
647	1/18	Burger Buster	$45.99		$1,121.68
648	1/19	Snipper Salon	$13.67		$1,108.01
649	1/20	Ring-A-Ling	$144.91		$963.10
650	1/20	Walkin' Wear	$56.00		$907.10
651	1/20	Auto Al	$478.23		$428.87
652	1/21	Harry's Hats	$30.99		$397.88
	1/21	bonus check		$675.25	$1,073.13

CW14 Challenge

Name _____

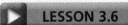

Popular Hot Spots

Many people like the warm weather in the state of Florida.
Listed below are the populations for major cities in Florida.

Florida Cities	City Population
Fort Lauderdale	153,728
Hialeah	211,392
Jacksonville	693,630
Miami	368,624
Orlando	181,175
St. Petersburg	236,029
Tallahassee	136,628
Tampa	289,156

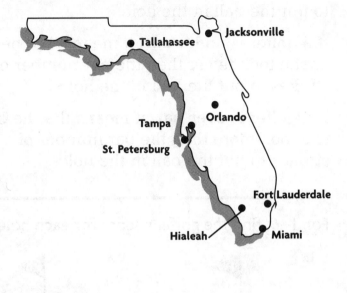

Tell if an estimate or exact answer is needed. Solve.

1. What is the difference in population between Hialeah and Orlando?

   _____
   exact; 30,217 people

2. Which three cities have a total population about the same as
   Jacksonville?

   _____
   estimate; possible answer: St. Petersburg,

   _____
   Fort Lauderdale, and Tampa

3. The cities of Tampa and St. Petersburg share an airport. Do you think
   that the Tampa-St. Petersburg airport would be larger than the
   Jacksonville airport? Explain.

   _____
   estimate; no, Tampa and St. Petersburg total about

   _____
   500,000 people. Jacksonville is much larger

   _____
   with 693,630.

4. How many more people live in Fort Lauderdale than in Tallahassee?

   _____
   exact; 17,100 people

Challenge   CW15

Par for the Course

In golf the **par** for a hole is the number of strokes, or hits, it takes an average golfer to put the ball in the hole.

If a golfer is **under par**, it means that he or she took fewer than the par number of strokes to put the ball in the hole.

If a golfer is **over par**, it means that he or she took more than the par number of strokes to put the ball in the hole.

> par for the hole: 4
> golfer's strokes: 1 under par
> golfer's score: $4 - 1 = 3$
>
> par for the hole: 4
> golfer's strokes: 2 over par
> golfer's score: $4 + 2 = 6$

For 1–6, find the golfer's score for each hole.

1.

Par: 3
Strokes: 1 under par

Score: __2__

2.
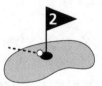

Par: 4
Strokes: 1 under par

Score: __3__

3.
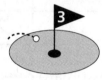

Par: 3
Strokes: 1 over par

Score: __4__

4.

Par: 2
Strokes: par

Score: __2__

5.

Par: 3
Strokes: 2 over par

Score: __5__

6.

Par: 5
Strokes: 2 under par

Score: __3__

7. a. Add the par numbers for the holes to find the par for the course.

   Par for the course: __20__

   b. Add the golfer's scores for the holes to find her or his score for the course.

   Score for the course: __19__

   c. Was the golfer over or under par for the course? By how much?

   __under par; 1 stroke__

CW16 Challenge

Triangle Sums

The sum along each side of the triangle is the same.
Use the properties of addition to help you find the missing numbers.

The sum is 10.

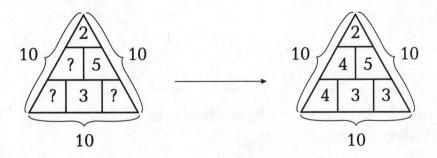

Find the missing numbers.

1. Sum is 12.

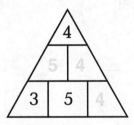

2. Sum is 15.

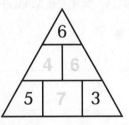

3. Sum is 18.

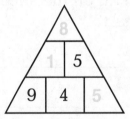

4. Sum is 25.

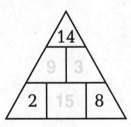

5. Sum is 33.

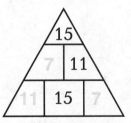

6. Sum is 49.

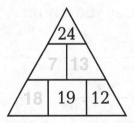

7. Sum is 65.

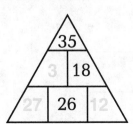

8. Sum is 78.

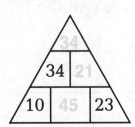

9. Sum is 100.

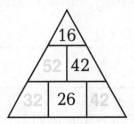

Equation Challenge

Write and solve an equation for each of the following. Choose a variable for the unknown number. Possible answers are shown:

1. There are 20 channels available on the TV. Five are local. How many are not local?

   _____
   $20 = 5 + n; n = 15$
   _____

2. There are 17 children in the class. Five more students join the class. How many students are in the class?

   _____
   $17 + 5 = n; n = 22$
   _____

3. Eight books were removed from the shelf. Three books are still on the shelf. How many books were on the shelf to start?

   _____
   $n - 8 = 3; n = 11$
   _____

4. Thomas had $50 in his bank account. After he withdrew some money, he had $35 left in his account. How much money did Thomas withdraw?

   _____
   $\$50 - n = \$35; n = \$15$
   _____

5. There are 15 members at the club meeting. After some more members join them, there are 24 members at the meeting. How many members joined the meeting?

   _____
   $15 + n = 24; n = 9$
   _____

Name _____

Find a Rule

Complete the table using the given rule.

1. $a + b = 7$

a	b
7	0
4	3
5	2
3	4

2. $a - 5 = b$

a	b
5	0
24	19
16	11
51	46

3. $3 \times a = b$

a	b
2	6
4	12
5	15
0	0

Find a rule for the output values. Write the rule as an equation that includes variables a and b. Possible answers are given.

4. Output b: 5, 7, 9, 11 _____ $a + 2 = b$ _____

5. Output b: 10, 7, 4, 1 _____ $a - 3 = b$ _____

6. Output b: 6, 12, 24, 48 _____ $2 \times a = b$ _____

Write a sequence for the rule. Possible answers shown.

7. $a - 4 = b$ _____ 54, 50, 46, 42 _____

8. $a + (2 - 1) = b$ _____ 25, 26, 27, 28 _____

9. $a - (3 - 3) = b$ _____ any number such as 5, 6, and 7 _____

10. $a + (4 - 3) = b$ _____ 18, 19, 20, 21 _____

11. $(a + 2) - 2 = b$ _____ any number such as 1, 2, and 3 _____

12. $(a + 4) - (2 + 1) = b$ _____ 5, 6, 7, 8 _____

Balance It

Write the expressions from the box below above the pans of the balances so that the two amounts on a balance are the same.

8 + 9	7 + 7	3 + 8	20 − 6
5 + 6	12 − 4	15 + 0	9 − 1
11 + 6	18 − 3	9 + 9	14 − 2
11 + 7	6 + 6	17 − 8	13 − 4

Possible answers are shown.

1. __7 + 7__   __20 − 6__

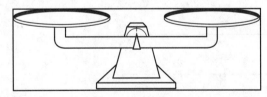

2. __8 + 9__   __11 + 6__

3. __12 − 4__   __9 − 1__

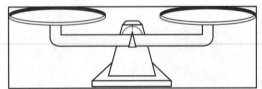

4. __15 + 0__   __18 − 3__

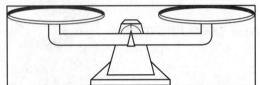

5. __3 + 8__   __5 + 6__

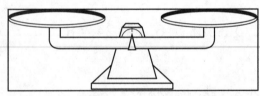

6. __6 + 6__   __14 − 2__

7. __13 − 4__   __17 − 8__

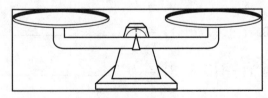

8. __9 + 9__   __11 + 7__

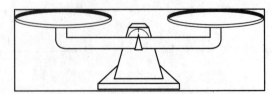

Deciphering the King's Numbers

You and your friends visit the ruins of an ancient civilization. There are many stone tablets carved with English words, but the numbers are in strange symbols. So far, no one can decode the symbols. Can you?

There are four number symbols: $\diamond$, $\square$, $\bigcirc$, and $\triangle$.

Passage 1: "The King has $\diamond$ grandsons, together they have 6 knees."

Passage 2: "Every birthday the King gives his daughter $\diamond$ more flowers compared to the previous year. This year he gave her $\diamond + \bigcirc$ flowers. Last year she got $\diamond + \triangle$ flowers."

Passage 3: "The King has $\diamond \times \diamond$ horses. That is $\diamond$ more than the Prince's $\diamond \times \square$ horses."

1. What number does $\diamond$ represent?

   3

2. Which digit is greater, $\bigcirc$ or $\triangle$?

   O

3. What is $(\diamond + \bigcirc) - (\diamond + \triangle)$?

   3

4. How many horses does the Prince have?

   6 horses

5. What is $\square$?

   2

Make up your own code of symbols for the digits 0, 1, 2, 3, 4, 5, 6, 7, 8, and 9. Write 3 of your symbols in several different expressions. Ask a friend to decode your 3 symbols.

Answers will vary.

_____

_____

_____

_____

_____

Stop That Watch!

Work with a partner to estimate and then check how many times you can do different activities in one minute.

You need a watch with a second hand.

1. Record your estimates and findings in the tables. Answers will vary.

Partner 1 Name _____   Partner 2 Name _____

Activity	Estimated Number of Repetitions	Actual Number of Repetitions
Write your name.		
Hop on one foot.		
Draw a star and color it.		
Walk around your desk or table.		
Count to 200.		

Activity	Estimated Number of Repetitions	Actual Number of Repetitions
Write your name.		
Hop on one foot.		
Draw a star and color it.		
Walk around your desk or table.		
Count to 200.		

2. How close are the actual numbers to your estimated numbers? Write a paragraph to explain. Check students' answers.

_____

_____

_____

_____

Name _____

Replace the Batteries

Mr. Smith checked the time on all of the clocks in his shop before leaving work at 8:00 P.M. on Monday. On Tuesday morning he noticed that some of the clocks were running slow. He realized that he needed to replace the batteries in those clocks and reset the time.

The exact time is 7:30 A.M. Write how much time each clock has lost. Use the abbreviations *hr* and *min*.

1.

_____2 hr 25 min_____

2.

_____5 min_____

3.

_____1 hr 2 min_____

4.

_____11 hr 25 min_____

5.

_____8 hr 39 min_____

6.

_____4 hr 52 min_____

7.

_____3 hr 18 min_____

8.

_____4 hr 4 min_____

Name _____

Trina's Tuesday

Read the following story about Trina's Tuesday. Then make an ordered list of the 15 things that happened to Trina, starting at 2:00 A.M. Tuesday and continuing until 11:00 P.M. Wednesday.

Trina woke up to the sound of her alarm clock at 6:00 A.M. She felt tired because a thunder storm woke her up at 2:00 A.M. She ate breakfast at 7:00 A.M. and took the bus at 8:00 A.M. On the bus Trina studied for her Math test, which was at 2:00 P.M.

She arrived at school at 9:00 A.M. The teacher told Trina that there was an assembly at 1:00 P.M. Trina did Social Studies at 10:00 A.M., and at 12:00 P.M., she ate lunch.

At 3:00 P.M. she took the bus home. Dinner was at 6:00 P.M. Trina was happy that she had done all of her homework at 4:00 P.M. so she was able to play outside at 7:00 P.M. At 9:00 P.M., Trina went to sleep. She heard her baby brother cry at 11:00 P.M. but went right back to sleep.

1. 2:00 A.M. thunder storm
2. 6:00 A.M. alarm clock
3. 7:00 A.M. breakfast
4. 8:00 A.M. bus
5. 9:00 A.M. arrive at school
6. 10:00 A.M. Social Studies
7. 12:00 P.M. lunch
8. 1:00 P.M. assembly
9. 2:00 P.M. Math test
10. 3:00 P.M. bus home
11. 4:00 P.M. homework
12. 6:00 P.M. dinner
13. 7:00 P.M. play outside
14. 9:00 P.M. went to sleep
15. 11:00 P.M. brother cries

Name _____

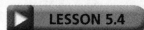

Hatching Eggs

The table shows the average incubation time for eggs of different kinds of birds. Incubation time is the number of days between the time an egg is laid and the time it hatches.

INCUBATION TIME FOR EGGS	
Kind of Bird	**Average Number of Days**
Chicken	21
Duck	30
Turkey	26
Goose	30

For Problems 1–6, use the table and a calendar.

1. How much longer does it usually take a duck's egg to hatch than a chicken's egg? _____9 days_____

2. If a chicken lays an egg on June 1, on about what date should the egg hatch? ____about June 22 if we count June 2 as day 1____

3. If a duck lays an egg on June 21, on about what date should the egg hatch? _____about July 21_____

4. A turkey egg hatches on July 4. On about what date was the turkey egg laid? _____about June 8_____

5. A goose egg hatches on the last day in July. On about what date was the goose egg laid? _____about July 1_____

6. A chick is 3 days old on July 31. On what date did the chicken egg hatch? ____July 28 if the chick is 0 days old on its day of birth____

   On about what date was the egg laid? _____about July 7_____

Find the Missing Data

The Lane family drove their car on vacation. At the end of each day, Mr. Lane recorded the number of miles that they had driven.

1. Complete the table to find out how far the Lanes traveled each day.

Day	Miles in One Day	Total Miles (Cumulative Frequency)
Monday	150 mi	150 miles
Tuesday	75 mi	225 miles
Wednesday	143 mi	368 miles
Thursday	10 mi	378 miles
Friday	122 mi	500 miles
Saturday	75 mi	575 miles

Matt took a notebook on the trip. He used the notebook to draw pictures and play games with his sister.

2. Look at the table below. How many notebook pages did

   Matt use by the end of the trip? _____ 80 pages _____

3. Complete the table to find out how many pages Matt used on each day of the trip.

Day	Pages in One Day	Total Pages (Cumulative Frequency)
Monday	20 pages	20 pages
Tuesday	13 pages	33 pages
Wednesday	12 pages	45 pages
Thursday	28 pages	73 pages
Friday	7 pages	80 pages
Saturday	0 pages	80 pages

Find the Mean, the Median, and the Mode

1. What numbers are missing from this group?
   The mode is 10 and the median is 9.

   4, 4, 6, 8, __9__, 10, 10, __10__, 11

For 2–7, use the table at right. Pay close attention to each question. The mean, median, and mode of the grades are different from the mean, median, and mode of the number of students.

RECYCLING CLUB MEMBERS	
Grade	Number of Students
1	7
2	5
4	5
5	3

2. What is the median grade of students in the recycling club?

   _____3_____

3. What is the median number of students from each grade in the recycling club?

   _____5 students_____

4. What grade is the mode?

   _____there is no mode_____

5. What number of students is the mode?

   _____5_____

6. What is the mean number of students from each grade in the recycling club?

   _____5 students_____

7. Suppose four more fourth graders join the club.
   a. Does the mode of the number of students change? Explain.

   _____Yes, there is now no mode._____

   b. Does the median number of students change? Explain.

   _____Yes, the median increases to 6._____

   c. Does the mean number of students change? Explain.

   _____Yes, the mean increases to 6._____

Challenge   CW27

Line Plot

Stephanie is comparing the number of letters in her classmates' first names. She printed each student's name on a piece of paper. She then began to count and record the number of letters in each name.

1. Complete Stephanie's line plot by recording the number of letters in the first names of the other students in her class.

Jennifer	Zachary	Lee	Elizabeth	Dimitri
Ted	Inderjeet	Trudi	Malcolm	Lauren
Carl	Koko	Matthew	Moe	Kathleen
Juan	Joanie	Christopher	Oscar	Ramona
Paul	Siri	Mercedes	Kevin	Alan

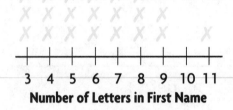

```
        X
        X
        X           X
X   X   X   X   X   X
X   X   X   X   X   X   X
X   X   X   X   X   X   X       X
+---+---+---+---+---+---+---+---+
3   4   5   6   7   8   9  10  11
```
Number of Letters in First Name

For 2–5, use the completed line plot.

2. How many first names have 7 letters?

_____4_____

3. What is the most frequent number of letters in a first

   name in Stephanie's class? _____4 letters_____

4. What is the range of this data? _____8_____

5. Would the data be different if you made a line plot for the number of letters in the first names of students in your class? Make a list of names and a line plot for your classmates.

```
+---+---+---+---+---+---+---+---+---+
2   3   4   5   6   7   8   9  10  11
```
Number of Letters in First Name

_____Yes; check students' work._____

Name _____

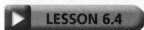

How Many Marbles in a Jar?

Mr. Murphy asked each of the students in his class to estimate the number of marbles in a jar. He organized the estimates in a stem-and-leaf plot.

Marble Estimates

Stem	Leaves
6	3 5 5 6 7
7	0 0 0 4 4 5 8 9 9
8	0 3 3 6 6
9	0 5

6 | 3 means 63 marbles.

For 1–4, use the stem-and-leaf plot.

1. What number was estimated by the greatest number of students?

   _____ 70 _____

2. What is the median in this set of estimates?

   _____ 75 _____

3. What is the difference between the highest estimate and

   the lowest estimate? _____ 32 _____

4. Use the following clues and the stem-and-leaf plot to determine the exact number of marbles in the jar.

   • Only one student guessed the exact number.

   • The exact number is not a multiple of 5.

   • The exact number has 7 tens.

   There are exactly _____ 78 _____ marbles in the jar.

Name _____

Did You Know?

The table shows the
oldest recorded age
of some animals.

Animal	Age (in years)
Cat	28
Dog	20
Goat	18
Rabbit	13
Guinea Pig	8
Mouse	6

Use the data in the table above to complete the graph. Draw bars
across the graph to show the age of each animal.

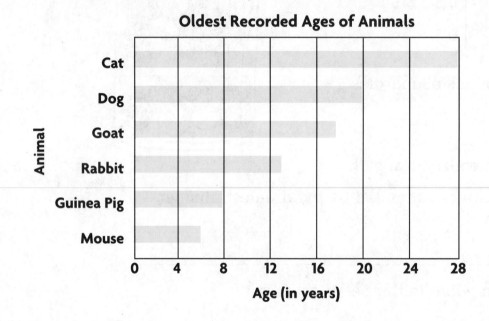

Oldest Recorded Ages of Animals

1. What interval is used in the scale of the graph?

   4

2. For which animals do the bars end exactly on the scale lines?

   cat, dog, guinea pig

3. If the graph had a scale with intervals of 2, how many
   bars would end exactly on the scale lines?

   5 bars

CW30   Challenge

Use Graphic Aids

Students collected empty soda cans.
The amounts collected are shown in the table.

SODA CANS COLLECTED	
Monday	40
Tuesday	35
Wednesday	25
Thursday	15
Friday	20

1. What is the range of the data in the table? ____25____

2. In a pictograph of this data, suppose you chose a soda can as a symbol. You want each symbol to represent whole cans in the graph. What amount could the symbol represent, other than 1? ____Each can = 5 cans collected____

3. Using your answer to 2, make a pictograph of the data in the table.

Check students' pictographs. Possible graph below.

SODA CANS COLLECTED	
Day	Number of Cans
Monday	🥫 🥫 🥫 🥫 🥫 🥫 🥫 🥫
Tuesday	🥫 🥫 🥫 🥫 🥫 🥫 🥫
Wednesday	🥫 🥫 🥫 🥫 🥫
Thursday	🥫 🥫 🥫
Friday	🥫 🥫 🥫 🥫
Each 🥫 = 5 cans collected	

4. On which two consecutive days did the students collect the most cans?

_____Monday and Tuesday_____

5. When would it be easier to use a graph instead of a table to find an answer?

_____Possible answer: When you want to visually_____

_____compare amounts._____

6. When would it be easier to use a table instead of a graph to find an answer?

_____Possible answer: When you want to calculate_____

_____with exact numbers._____

Strike Up the Band

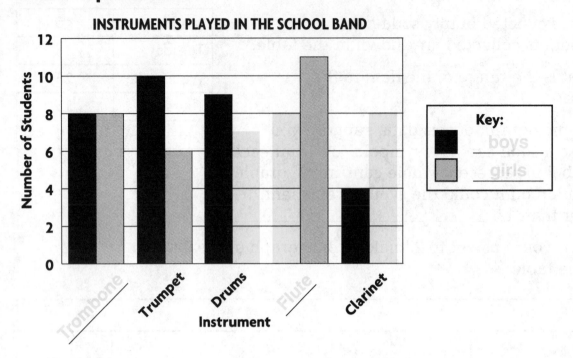

INSTRUMENTS PLAYED IN THE SCHOOL BAND

Key:
■ ___boys___
▨ ___girls___

1. Use the clues to fill in the missing information on this double-bar graph.

   • The same number of boys and girls play the trombone.

   • More boys than girls play the trumpet.

   • Two more boys than girls play the drums.

   • More girls play the flute than any other instrument.

   • The same number of boys play the flute and the trombone.

   • Twice as many girls as boys play the clarinet.

For 2–5, use the completed graph.

2. Which instruments are played by more boys than girls?

   _____trumpet and drums_____

3. Do more students play the flute or the trumpet? _____flute_____

4. Are there more boys or more girls in the band? _____girls_____

5. How many students are in the band? _____79 students_____

Temperature Patterns

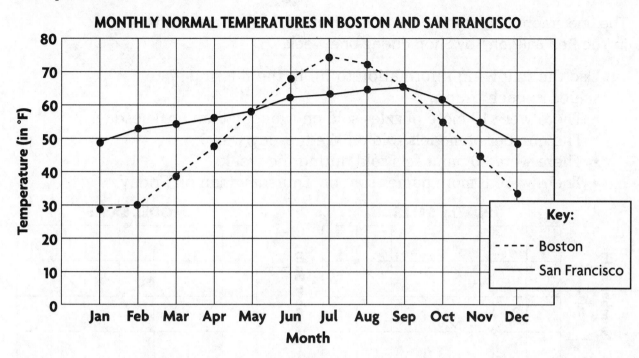

MONTHLY NORMAL TEMPERATURES IN BOSTON AND SAN FRANCISCO

Key:
- - - - Boston
——— San Francisco

This line graph shows the normal temperatures in Boston and San Francisco for each month of the year.

1. What does the dashed line represent?

normal temperatures in Boston

_____

2. What is normally the coldest month in Boston?

January

_____

3. What is normally the warmest month in San Francisco?

September

_____

4. In which city is the difference in temperature between the summer months and the winter months greater?

Boston

_____

5. During which months is the normal temperature in the two cities the same?

May and September

_____

Name _____

Find the Missing Scales

The line graphs below show the number of sales of several items in The Red Balloon Toy Shop during one week.

1. Use the following information to fill in the missing scales in each graph.
   - There were 10 more puzzles sold on Monday than on Tuesday.
   - The number of models sold on Wednesday was 5.
   - There were 60 paint sets sold during the week.
   - There were 8 more games sold on Thursday than on Friday.

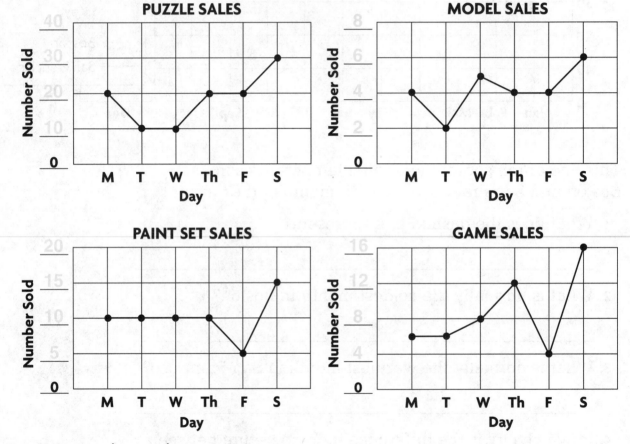

For 2–5, use the graphs.

2. How many models were sold in all during the week? _____ 25 models

3. On which day was the greatest number of paint sets sold? _____ Saturday

4. Were there more sales of models or games on Monday? _____ games

5. Write two more similar questions using the data in the graphs.

_____ Check students' questions. _____

CW34   Challenge

Name _____

Blast from the Past

A total of 80 fourth-grade students at Forest Elementary School took a field trip to the history museum. During the trip, the students visited either the *Mummies* exhibit, the *Knights and Castles* exhibit, the *Dinosaurs* exhibit, or the *Wild West* exhibit.

1. Use the clues to fill in the missing labels on the circle graph to show how many students visited each exhibit.

   • More students visited the *Mummies* exhibit than any other exhibit.

   • The same number of students visited the *Knights and Castles* exhibit as visited the *Wild West* exhibit.

   • Twice as many students visited the *Dinosaurs* exhibit as visited the *Knights and Castles* exhibit.

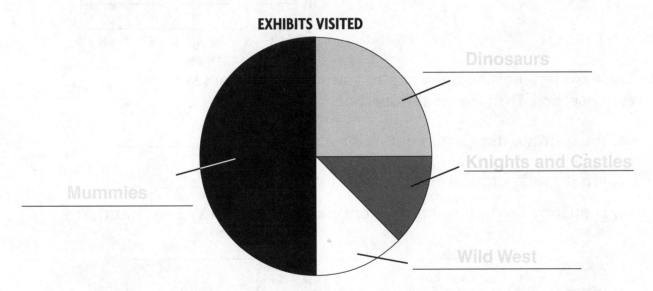

EXHIBITS VISITED

For 2–3, use the completed graph.

2. How many students visited each exhibit?

   Mummies, 40 students; Dinosaurs, 20 students; Knights

   and Castles, 10 students; Wild West, 10 students

3. How many students in all visited the *Mummies* exhibit and the *Knights and Castles* exhibit?

   50 students

Challenge CW35

Data Display

Corina recorded the grades that she got on her spelling
test each week for nine weeks. She displayed the data in
two different ways.

A

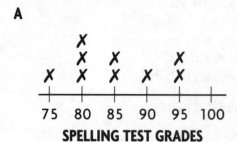

SPELLING TEST GRADES

B

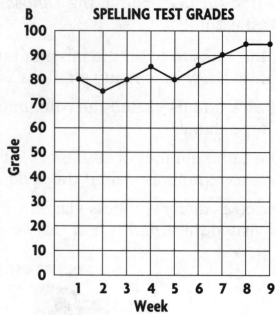

SPELLING TEST GRADES

Circle the letter of the graph or plot you would use to answer
each question. Then answer the question.

1. What grade did Corina get most often? (A) B _____80_____

2. What grade did Corina get in Week 5? A (B) _____80_____

3. Did Corina's grades improve or decline between Weeks 5 and 8?

    A (B) _____improve_____

4. What is the range of Corina's grades? A B _____20 points_____

    _____Possible answers: A, B, or both_____

5. By how many points did Corina's grade improve between Weeks 2 and 3?

    A (B) _____by 5 points_____

6. What is the median of Corina's grades? A B _____85 points_____

    _____Possible answers: A, B, or both_____

What's the Reason?

The graph at the right shows the number of students enrolled at Kensington Elementary in 7 different years.

When we read a graph, we can make conclusions about what happened, then try to think of reasons why those things might have happened.

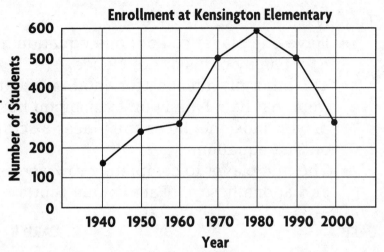

Enrollment at Kensington Elementary

For example:

Conclusion: The number of students enrolled at Kensington Elementary rose steadily between 1940, 1950, and 1960.

Possible Reason: The community around the school was growing steadily, meaning that there were more children to attend Kensington Elementary.

Give a possible reason for each of the following conclusions. Answers may vary. Possible answers given.

1. **Conclusion:** There was a sharp increase in the number of students between 1960 and 1970.

   Possible Reason:

   Possible answers: The school built an addition; a new

   housing development was built near the school.

2. **Conclusion:** The number of students enrolled at Kensington Elementary began to decrease steadily after 1980.

   Possible Reason:

   Possible answer: Another school opened nearby.

   _____

   _____

Fact Family Bingo

Master basic multiplication facts with a friendly game of
Fact Family Bingo. Play with several students.

Check students' answers as they play.

To play:
- Have one player call out one equation from the
  Fact Family of his or her choice.
- The other players look for another equation
  from that Fact Family on their bingo board. If a
  player finds one, he or she places a scrap of paper
  on that equation.
- The first player to complete a row across, down,
  or diagonally says "Fact Family Bingo."

CARD A

$2 \times 3 = 6$	$4\overline{)12}$	$3\overline{)18}$	$4 \times 2 = 8$	$3 \times 3 = 9$
$5\overline{)25}$	$5 \times 4 = 20$	$2\overline{)16}$	$7 \times 2 = 14$	$2\overline{)4}$
$2\overline{)10}$	$3 \times 1 = 3$	FREE	$1\overline{)2}$	$3\overline{)15}$
$8\overline{)40}$	$7 \times 8 = 56$	$9\overline{)18}$	$6\overline{)48}$	$9 \times 9 = 81$
$12\overline{)60}$	$6\overline{)72}$	$9\overline{)90}$	$6\overline{)30}$	$6 \times 9 = 54$

CARD B

$11 \times 11 = 121$	$1 \times 1 = 1$	$12\overline{)144}$	$4\overline{)8}$	$3\overline{)9}$
$9\overline{)45}$	$8\overline{)80}$	$2 \times 6 = 12$	$8 \times 9 = 72$	$12\overline{)96}$
$9\overline{)99}$	$3\overline{)9}$	FREE	$1\overline{)3}$	$12\overline{)108}$
$5 \times 6 = 30$	$2 \times 12 = 24$	$6 \times 7 = 42$	$2 \times 7 = 14$	$12 \times 7 = 84$
$5 \times 9 = 45$	$7\overline{)63}$	$5 \times 7 = 35$	$7 \times 10 = 70$	$10 \times 10 = 100$

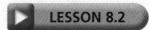

Name _____

Math Machinery

Each machine in Mariko's Machinery Shop does different things with the numbers put into it.

Complete the *In* and *Out* columns for each machine.

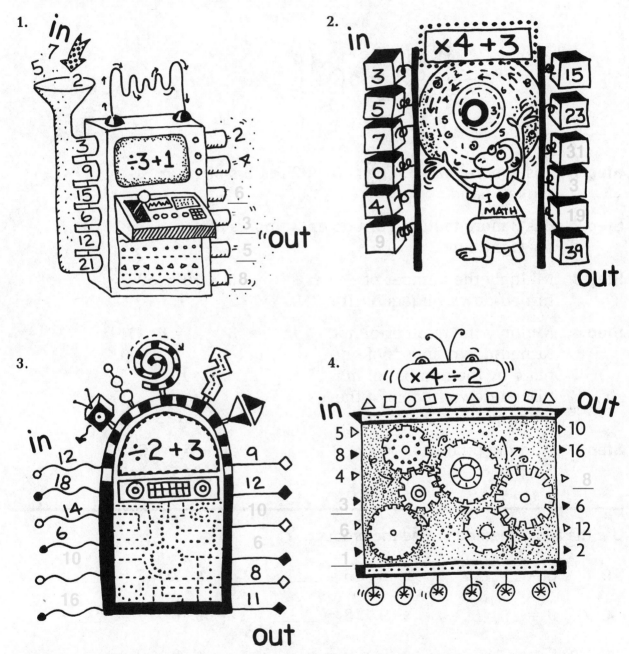

5. The machine in Problem 4 needs to be reprogrammed to do the same job in one step instead of two. How can this be done?

Have the machine multiply the number put into it by 2.

Fingers and Factors

Mickey's mother taught him how to multiply by using his fingers. She said this is a very old method. It only works when the factors are greater than 5. Here are the steps Mickey followed to find the product of 7 × 8.

Step 1 7 is 2 more than 5. Turn down 2 fingers of the left hand.

Step 2 8 is 3 more than 5. Turn down 3 fingers of the right hand.

Step 3 Multiply the number of turned-down fingers by 10. $5 \times 10 = 50$

Step 4 Multiply the number of *not* turned-down fingers of one hand by the number of *not* turned-down fingers of the other hand. $3 \times 2 = 6$

Step 5 Add the products. $50 + 6 = 56$
So, 7 × 8 = 56.

Use the above method to find the product.

1. 6 × 8 = __48__

2. 6 × 6 = __36__

3. 7 × 7 = __49__

4. 7 × 9 = __63__

5. 9 × 8 = __72__

6. 6 × 7 = __42__

7. 9 × 9 = __81__

8. 6 × 9 = __54__

9. 8 × 8 = __64__

10. 7 × 6 = __42__

11. 8 × 7 = __56__

12. 9 × 6 = __54__

13. 8 × 6 = __48__

14. 9 × 7 = __63__

15. 8 × 9 = __72__

CW40   Challenge

Number Connection

Decide how the numbers are related.
Think: Are you multiplying or dividing?
By what number are you multiplying or dividing?

EXAMPLE 1:

8 is to 24 as 6 is to _____.

$8 \times$ _____ $= 24$

$8 \times 3 = 24$, and $6 \times 3 = 18$.

So, 8 is to 24 as 6 is to 18.

EXAMPLE 2:

56 is to 7 as 16 is to _____.

$56 \div$ _____ $= 7$

$56 \div 8 = 7$, and $16 \div 8 = 2$.

So, 56 is to 7 as 16 is to 2.

Decide how the numbers are related. Use a multiplication table to help you. The first two are done for you.

1. 40 is to 4 as 90 is to __9__.
2. 7 is to 49 as 6 is to __42__.
3. 9 is to 72 as 11 is to __88__.
4. 48 is to 6 as 56 is to __7__.
5. 120 is to 10 as 108 is to __9__.
6. 11 is to 121 as 7 is to __77__.
7. 8 is to 72 as 7 is to __63__.
8. 7 is to 42 as 12 is to __72__.
9. 99 is to 11 as 72 is to __8__.
10. 84 is to 7 as 96 is to __8__.
11. 9 is to 81 as 12 is to __108__.
12. 132 is to 11 as 72 is to __6__.
13. 6 is to 48 as 10 is to __80__.
14. 7 is to 56 as 8 is to __64__.

Up, Down, or Diagonal

Find three numbers in a row that have the given product. Draw a line through the three numbers. You may draw the line across, up and down, or diagonally.

1. product: 36

1	2	5
6	3	0
7	6	2

2. product: 120

2	9	5
3	5	7
5	6	4

3. product: 90

7	2	9
3	5	1
2	4	9

4. product: 40

4	3	6
2	5	7
0	8	2

5. product: 96

7	4	5
2	8	6
6	4	3

6. product: 108

3	8	6
6	3	4
9	6	2

7. product: 96

5	3	4
4	2	8
7	9	3

8. product: 108

4	6	2
9	7	4
3	2	8

9. product: 84

7	6	2
1	4	7
9	5	8

10. product: 144

3	7	3
2	4	6
7	4	12

11. product: 84

4	5	3
8	0	7
6	9	4

12. product: 48

6	5	3
6	2	4
7	8	9

13. Make your own puzzle. Exchange with a partner to solve.

product: ___Answers will vary.___

Name _____

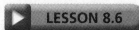

Birthday Greetings

Grandma Gallagher will soon be 75 years old. Her ten grandchildren made a card to give her on her birthday. They will sign their names in order from oldest to youngest.

Use the clues below to find the age of each grandchild. Record the names in the chart.

1. Ryan is 8 years old.

2. Nadia is 5 years younger than Ryan.

3. Nick is 6 times as old as Nadia.

4. Mary Kate is 4 years older than Ryan.

5. Emma is 2 years older than Nadia.

6. Charlotte is half as old as Mary Kate.

7. Jack is 4 times as old as Emma.

8. Margaret is 4 years older than Charlotte.

9. Laura is 7 years younger than Nick.

10. Michael is twice as old as Ryan.

For Problems 11–12, use the chart.

11. Who will sign the card first? last?

   _____ Jack; Nadia _____

12. Who will be the fifth person to

   sign the card? _____ Laura _____

20 yr ———— Jack ————

19 yr ————————————

18 yr ———— Nick ————

17 yr ————————————

16 yr ———— Michael ————

15 yr ————————————

14 yr ————————————

13 yr ————————————

12 yr ———— Mary Kate ————

11 yr ———— Laura ————

10 yr ———— Margaret ————

9 yr ————————————

8 yr ———— Ryan ————

7 yr ————————————

6 yr ———— Charlotte ————

5 yr ———— Emma ————

4 yr ————————————

3 yr ———— Nadia ————

More Expressions

You can write expressions to match the words in difficult problems. Then you can find the value of the expression to solve the problem.

Example: There are 6 boxes with 4 markers in each box and 3 boxes with 5 markers in each box. How many markers are there in all?

Expression: $(6 \times 4) + (3 \times 5)$ ← Do the operations in parentheses first.
Find the value: 24 + 15
                     39

So, there are 39 markers in all.

___

Write an expression that matches the words. Then use the expression to solve the problem.

1. Rebecca has 6 pages of trading cards. There are 9 cards on each page. She gives 2 pages of the cards to her brother. How many cards does she have left?

   $(6 \times 9) - (2 \times 9)$; 36 cards

2. What is the total cost for 4 concert tickets that cost $12 each and 6 tickets that cost $8 each?

   $(4 \times 12) + (6 \times 8)$; $96

3. The teacher divided 50 pencils equally among 5 boxes. Then she put 2 pens and 1 eraser in each box. How many items are in each box?

   $(50 \div 5) + 2 + 1$; 13 items

4. There are 5 cars with 4 people in each car and 2 vans with 8 people in each van. How many people are there in all?

   $(5 \times 4) + (2 \times 8)$; 36 people

Operation Match

0	5	6	1	7
9	11	12	13	15
17	24	45	30	

Match the value of each expression with a value from the box above. Some numbers may be used more than once.

1. $(8 \times 4) - 6 \div 3$ _____30_____

2. $7 + 5 - 12 \div 4$ _____9_____

3. $20 \div (9 - 5) + 1$ _____6_____

4. $27 \div 9 + 5 - 1$ _____7_____

5. $6 \times 4 \div (3 - 1)$ _____12_____

6. $(6 \times 4) \div 3 - 1$ _____7_____

7. $20 \div 4 - 2 - 3$ _____0_____

8. $20 \div 4 - (2 + 3)$ _____0_____

9. $7 + 7 \div 7 + 3$ _____11_____

10. $(7 + 7) \div 7 + 3$ _____5_____

11. $(4 + 5) \times (2 + 3)$ _____45_____

12. $4 + 5 \times 2 + 3$ _____17_____

13. $9 + 4 - 2 \times 3$ _____7_____

14. $9 + (4 - 2) \times 3$ _____15_____

Name _____

Solve the Equation

Write an equation using a variable. Tell what the variable
represents. Then use mental math to solve the equation.

Equations and variables may vary. Possible equations are shown.

1. A number of eggs in 5 cartons is 3 eggs in each carton.
How many eggs are there?

   $n \div 5 = 3$; n = number of eggs;

   $n = 15$ eggs

2. 6 chairs at each of some tables is 42 chairs. How many
tables are there?

   $6 \times t = 42$; t = number of tables;

   $t = 7$ tables

3. A number of desks divided into 6 rows is 5 desks in each
row. How many desks are there?

   $d \div 6 = 5$; d = number of desks;

   $d = 30$ desks

4. 2 socks in each of some number of pairs of socks is
24 socks. How many pairs of socks are there?

   $2 \times p = 24$; p = number of pairs of socks;

   $p = 12$ pairs of socks

5. A number of soccer balls divided among 8 teams is
3 balls for each team. How many soccer balls are there?

   $s \div 8 = 3$; s = number of soccer balls;

   $s = 24$ soccer balls

6. 10 players on each of some basketball teams is 60 basketball players. How many teams are there?

   $10 \times t = 60$; t = number of teams;

   $t = 6$ teams

CW46 Challenge

Flying Around

Marty the Fly is standing on the grid below. When he flies, it is always one whole space either straight up, straight down, directly left, or directly right.

Follow Marty's moves and tell where he lands.

Marty makes the following moves:

Starting in space D8, Marty moves 2 spaces up, 3 spaces right, 4 spaces left, 5 spaces up, 3 spaces right, 2 spaces down, 3 spaces right, 1 space up, and 2 spaces left.

	A	B	C	D	E	F	G	H	I	J
1										
2										
3										
4										
5										
6										
7										
8										
9										
10										

1. Where does Marty land? _____ space G2 _____

2. Make up your own moves for Marty, and have a friend play your game. Check students' games.

Keep It Equal

When the same amount of weight is on each side of a scale, the scale is balanced. If there is more weight on one side, the scale will tip to that side.

Use the information to balance the scale.

1 ○ weighs 1 pound.

1 □ weighs 2 pounds.

1 △ weighs 3 pounds.

1 △ + 4 ○ = 7 pounds, and 3□ + 1○ = 7 pounds.

So, the scale is balanced.

Tell how to make the scales balance. Possible answers are given.

1.

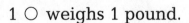

Add five pounds to the right
_____
side by adding 5 circles.

2.

Add one pound to the left side
_____
by adding one circle.

3.

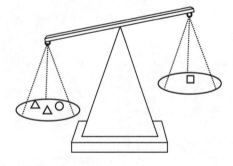

Add four pounds to the right
_____
side by adding 2 squares.

4.

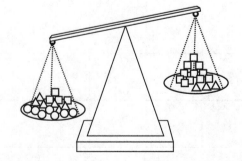

Add 2 pounds to the right side
_____
by adding 2 circles.

CW48   Challenge

Name _____

Play by the Rules

An input/output table can have any kind of rule.
Sometimes a rule is one step, like *multiply by 4*.

Sometimes a rule is two steps. Can you find a rule for the
input/output table?

Input	Output
3	10
5	14
6	16
10	24

Think: What operations on 3 give a value of 10?

Idea: Multiply by 3, then add 1.

Test your idea for input 5.
Does (5 × 3) + 1 = 14? no

Try again: Multiply by 2, then add 4.

Test your idea for input 5.
Does (5 × 2) + 4 = 14? yes

Test your idea for input 6.
Does (6 × 2) + 4 = 16? yes

Test your idea for input 10.
Does (10 × 2) + 4 = 24? yes

So, a rule for the input/output table is *multiply by 2, then
add 4.*

Find a rule for each input/output table. Remember, you must test
your rule on each row!

1.

Input	Output
3	9
4	11
8	19
10	23

multiply by 2, then add 3

2.

Input	Output
20	14
16	12
8	8
10	9

divide by 2, then add 4

The Powers That Be

You can write some greater numbers in a shorter form by using **exponents**. An exponent tells how many times to multiply a number, called the base, by itself.

$10^0 = 1$ base $\rightarrow 10^0$

$10^1 = 10$

$10^2 = 10 \times 10 = 100$

$10^3 = 10 \times 10 \times 10 = 1,000$

As you can see, the exponent also tells how many zeros follow the number 1.

Many scientists round greater numbers and use exponents.

One million equals 10^6. 18 million equals 18×10^6.

Draw a line to the matching number.

1. 32,000 •   • 89×10^5

2. 48,000,000 •   • 17×10^0

3. 560 •   • 9×10^6

4. 7,700 •   • 77×10^2

5. 8,900,000 •   • 32×10^3

6. 690,000 •   • 44×10^5

7. 9,000,000 •   • 16×10^7

8. 28,000 •   • 48×10^6

9. 17 •   • 98×10^6

10. 4,400,000 •   • 28×10^3

11. 160,000,000 •   • 56×10^1

12. 98,000,000 •   • 69×10^4

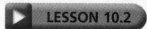

Name _____

About the Same

In each large box, circle all the sets of factors whose estimated product is the number in the center box.

1.

4×581	6×487	5×531
8×304	**2,400**	3×894
3×815	8×256	6×356

2.

3×999	5×555	6×456
6×601	**3,000**	5×499
5×648	6×666	3×1,845

3.

2×599	6×212	3×395
4×304	**1,200**	2×673
3×444	4×256	6×184

4.

6×524	4×888	9×444
4×973	**3,600**	6×555
9×381	6×631	4×918

5.

4×999	8×487	5×765
8×592	**4,000**	4×1,846
2×1,815	5×825	8×456

6.

2×8,344	4×3,456	8×1,793
4×4,444	**16,000**	2×7,891
8×2,468	2×8,500	4×4,567

7.

4×5,081	6×4,875	8×2,931
8×3,704	**24,000**	3×8,132
3×7,777	4×5,555	6×3,925

8.

5×6,872	3×9,999	6×4,721
6×4,382	**30,000**	5×5,734
6×5,377	5×6,294	3×10,388

Name _____

Missing Digits

In the multiplication problems below, one or two digits are missing. To find the missing digits, think of the basic multiplication facts.

Find the missing digits.

Example

$$\begin{array}{r} 3\,\boxed{} \\ \times\ 4 \\ \hline 1\ 2\ 8 \end{array}$$

Think: $4 \times \blacksquare = 8$

$4 \times 2 = 8$

$$\begin{array}{r} 3\ 2 \\ \times\ 4 \\ \hline 1\ 2\ 8 \end{array}$$

1.
$$\begin{array}{r} 1\,\boxed{5} \\ \times\ \ 3 \\ \hline 4\ 5 \end{array}$$

2.
$$\begin{array}{r} \boxed{1}\,6 \\ \times\ \ 4 \\ \hline 6\ 4 \end{array}$$

3.
$$\begin{array}{r} 1\ 9 \\ \times\ \ 2 \\ \hline 3\,\boxed{8} \end{array}$$

4.
$$\begin{array}{r} 2\,\boxed{7} \\ \times\ \ 4 \\ \hline 1\ 0\ 8 \end{array}$$

5.
$$\begin{array}{r} 1\ 1 \\ \times\ \boxed{5} \\ \hline 5\ 5 \end{array}$$

6.
$$\begin{array}{r} \boxed{1}\,3 \\ \times\ \ 3 \\ \hline 3\ 9 \end{array}$$

7.
$$\begin{array}{r} 2\ 3 \\ \times\ \ 4 \\ \hline \boxed{9}\,2 \end{array}$$

8.
$$\begin{array}{r} 2\ 1 \\ \times\ \ 5 \\ \hline 1\,\boxed{0}\,5 \end{array}$$

9.
$$\begin{array}{r} 3\,\boxed{4} \\ \times\ \ 2 \\ \hline 6\ 8 \end{array}$$

10.
$$\begin{array}{r} \boxed{5}\,9 \\ \times\ \ 4 \\ \hline 2\ 3\ 6 \end{array}$$

11.
$$\begin{array}{r} \boxed{4}\,5 \\ \times\ \ 3 \\ \hline 1\ 3\,\boxed{5} \end{array}$$

12.
$$\begin{array}{r} 5\,\boxed{8} \\ \times\ \ 6 \\ \hline \boxed{3}\,\boxed{4}\,8 \end{array}$$

13.
$$\begin{array}{r} 3\,\boxed{9} \\ \times\ \ 8 \\ \hline \boxed{3}\,\boxed{1}\,2 \end{array}$$

14.
$$\begin{array}{r} \boxed{2}\,7 \\ \times\ \ 9 \\ \hline 2\ 4\,\boxed{3} \end{array}$$

15.
$$\begin{array}{r} \boxed{4}\,2 \\ \times\ \ 7 \\ \hline 2\ 9\,\boxed{4} \end{array}$$

16.
$$\begin{array}{r} \boxed{8}\,6 \\ \times\ \ 3 \\ \hline 2\ 5\,\boxed{8} \end{array}$$

17.
$$\begin{array}{r} \boxed{5}\,1 \\ \times\ \ 4 \\ \hline \boxed{2}\,0\ 4 \end{array}$$

18.
$$\begin{array}{r} \boxed{7}\,4 \\ \times\ \ 8 \\ \hline 5\ 9\,\boxed{2} \end{array}$$

19.
$$\begin{array}{r} \boxed{6}\,3 \\ \times\ \ 6 \\ \hline 3\ 7\,\boxed{8} \end{array}$$

20.
$$\begin{array}{r} \boxed{8}\,8 \\ \times\ \ 8 \\ \hline 7\ 0\,\boxed{4} \end{array}$$

21.
$$\begin{array}{r} 2\,\boxed{9} \\ \times\ \ 2 \\ \hline \boxed{5}\,8 \end{array}$$

22.
$$\begin{array}{r} 8\,\boxed{7} \\ \times\ \ 6 \\ \hline \boxed{5}\,2\ 2 \end{array}$$

23.
$$\begin{array}{r} \boxed{6}\,1 \\ \times\ \ 7 \\ \hline 4\ 2\,\boxed{7} \end{array}$$

24.
$$\begin{array}{r} 4\,\boxed{8} \\ \times\ \ 5 \\ \hline \boxed{2}\,4\ 0 \end{array}$$

25.
$$\begin{array}{r} \boxed{6}\,8 \\ \times\ \ 9 \\ \hline 6\ 1\,\boxed{2} \end{array}$$

26.
$$\begin{array}{r} 8\,\boxed{9} \\ \times\ \ 4 \\ \hline \boxed{3}\,5\ 6 \end{array}$$

27.
$$\begin{array}{r} 3\,\boxed{7} \\ \times\ \ 9 \\ \hline \boxed{3}\,3\ 3 \end{array}$$

28.
$$\begin{array}{r} \boxed{3}\,5 \\ \times\ \ 7 \\ \hline 2\ 4\,\boxed{5} \end{array}$$

29.
$$\begin{array}{r} 7\,\boxed{2} \\ \times\ \ 8 \\ \hline \boxed{5}\,7\ 6 \end{array}$$

30.
$$\begin{array}{r} \boxed{5}\,4 \\ \times\ \ 6 \\ \hline 3\ 2\,\boxed{4} \end{array}$$

Multiply 3- and 4-Digit Numbers

Complete the multiplication puzzle.

246	×	4	=	984		621
×						×
3	×	2,157	=	6,471		4
=			×		=	

246 × 4 = 984 · 621

3 × 2,157 = 6,471 · 4

7 × 738 = 5,166 · 2 · 2,484

2

× 1,476

361 · 6 × 2,157 = 12,942 · 7 × 425 = 2,975

= 2,952

2,527 · 3,248 · 5 × 683 = 3,415

19,488 · 10,785 · 4 × 345 = 1,380

= 2,732 · × 5

8 · =

× 6,900

229 × 7 = 1,603

=

1,832

Name _____

Napier's Rods

John Napier, a Scottish mathematician, lived about 400 years ago. He invented the series of multiplication rods shown below.

Guide ×	0	1	2	3	4	5	6	7	8	9
1	0/0	0/1	0/2	0/3	0/4	0/5	0/6	0/7	0/8	0/9
2	0/0	0/2	0/4	0/6	0/8	1/0	1/2	1/4	1/6	1/8
3	0/0	0/3	0/6	0/9	1/2	1/5	1/8	2/1	2/4	2/7
4	0/0	0/4	0/8	1/2	1/6	2/0	2/4	2/8	3/2	3/6
5	0/0	0/5	1/0	1/5	2/0	2/5	3/0	3/5	4/0	4/5
6	0/0	0/6	1/2	1/8	2/4	3/0	3/6	4/2	4/8	5/4
7	0/0	0/7	1/4	2/1	2/8	3/5	4/2	4/9	5/6	6/3
8	0/0	0/8	1/6	2/4	3/2	4/0	4/8	5/6	6/4	7/2
9	0/0	0/9	1/8	2/7	3/6	4/5	5/4	6/3	7/2	8/1

You can use Napier's rods to multiply 4 × 5,370.

- Line up the guide rod and the rods for 5, 3, 7, and 0.
- Look at the numbers in the fourth row. Start at the right; add the numbers as shown. Then write them as shown.
- The answer is 21,480.

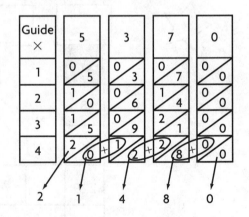

Copy or cut out the rods above. Use them to find the products.

1. 6 × 5,490 = _32,940_

2. 4 × 3,750 = _15,000_

3. 3 × 6,270 = _18,810_

4. 2 × 1,250 = _2,500_

5. 7 × 1,940 = _13,580_

6. 5 × 4,310 = _21,550_

CW54   Challenge

Name _____

Comparison Shopping

The music store offers CDs at $10.99 each or 5 for $44.95.
Which is the better deal?

- You can multiply the individual CD price by 5 to compare.
  $10.99 × 5 = $54.95 compared to 5 for $44.95.

The package deal for 5 CDs is the better buy.

Determine the better buy.

1. Fancy chocolate candies—
  14-piece box for $24.92 or
  each piece for $2.00?

  _____14-piece box_____

2. Batteries—
  2 for $1.57 or
  8 for $6.42?

  _____2 for $1.57_____

3. Eggs—
  $0.79 for 6 or
  $1.49 for 12?

  _____$1.49 for 12_____

4. Ice cream—
  1 half gallon for $1.89 or
  3 half gallons for $5.76?

  _____1 half gallon for $1.89_____

5. Coffee cups—
  1 for $0.89 or
  12 for $9.00?

  _____12 for $9.00_____

6. Butter—
  1 stick for $0.49 or
  4 sticks for $1.96?

  _____same price either way_____

7. Colored pencils—
  1 for $0.66 or
  6 for $4.10?

  _____1 for $0.66_____

8. Laundry detergent—
  64 oz for $2.99 or
  128 oz for $5.99?

  _____64 oz for $2.99_____

9. Spring water—
  1.5 liter for $1.69 or
  3.0 liter for $2.99?

  _____3.0 liter for $2.99_____

10. Candy bars—
  4 for $2.96 or
  12 for $8.40?

  _____12 for $8.40_____

Name _____

Moving Day

The Barretts are moving. Help them color code their boxes.
Solve the problems. Look at the number of zeros in the product.
Use the table below to color code the Barretts' boxes.

red	blue	yellow	yellow
40	400	20,000	6,000
× 20	× 20	× 40	× 300
800	8,000	800,000	1,800,000

blue	orange	orange	yellow	red
300	500	700	1,000	200
× 40	× 60	× 300	× 500	× 4
12,000	30,000	210,000	500,000	800

red	blue	blue	orange
900	400	4,000	500
× 6	× 30	× 4	× 300
5,400	12,000	16,000	150,000

orange	green	blue	red	yellow
80,000	60,000	700	800	90,000
× 4	× 50	× 30	× 3	× 20
320,000	3,000,000	21,000	2,400	1,800,000

Number of Zeros in Product	2	3	4	5	6
Color	red	blue	orange	yellow	green

CW56   Challenge

Cross-Number Puzzle

Look at how this cross-number puzzle illustrates the Distributive Property.

Use the puzzle to solve $7 \times 4 = n$.

Step 1 Write each factor in a rectangle.

Step 2 Break each factor into 2 of its addends. For example, $7 = 5 + 2$ and $4 = 3 + 1$. Write the addends (5 and 2 for 7) along the top and (3 and 1 for 4) along the right side of the puzzle.

7	5	2
			3
			1
◯		+	4

Step 3 Multiply the addends to fill in the inner boxes of the puzzle.

$5 \times 3 = 15$ $2 \times 3 = 6$
$5 \times 1 = 5$ $2 \times 1 = 2$

7	5	2
	15	6	3
	5	2	1
◯		+	4

Step 4 Add the products.
* Add the products horizontally and record the sums along the left side of the puzzle.

$15 + 6 = 21$
$5 + 2 = 7$

7	5	2
21	15	6	3
7	5	2	1
◯	20 + 8		4

* Add the products vertically and record the sums along the bottom of the puzzle.

$15 + 5 = 20$
$6 + 2 = 8$

Step 5 Add the sums.
$21 + 7 = 28$ and $20 + 8 = 28$
They should be equal. Record the sum in the circle. This is the product of 7×4.
So, $7 \times 4 = 28$.

7	5	2
21	15	6	3
7	5	2	1
28	20 + 8		4

Complete the cross-number puzzles.

1. $8 \times 5 = n$

8	2	6
16	4	12	2
24	6	18	3
40	10 + 30		5

2. $9 \times 6 = n$

9	4	5
27	12	15	3
27	12	15	3
54	24 + 30		6

Challenge **CW57**

Multiple Wheels

The factor in the outer circle times the factor in the inner circle equals the product in the center.

Write the missing multiples of 10.

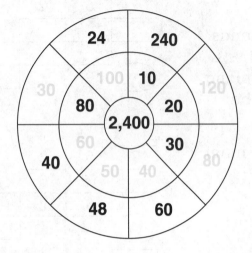

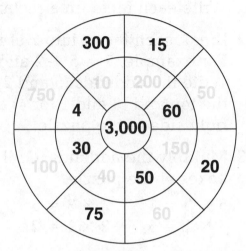

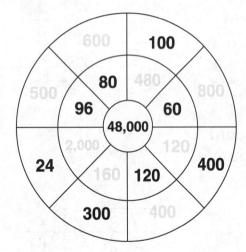

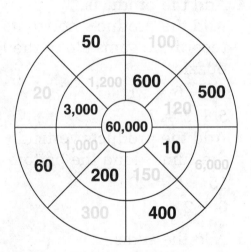

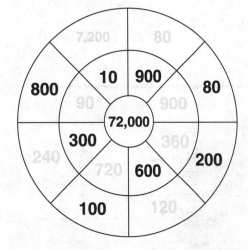

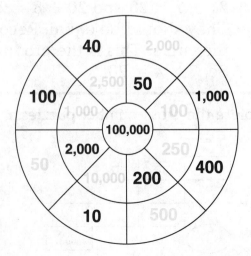

Name _____

On Target

Practice your estimation skills in this challenging game.

The object of the game is to choose a factor that produces a product closer to the chosen target.

Work with a partner to solve. Check students' work.

List A Product			List B Factor		
473	698	5,444	23	72	49
541	237	629	41	61	27
812	1,010	303	18	36	54
349	421	568	32	15	45

Step 1 One player chooses a number from List A as the target and circles it.

Step 2 The partner chooses a number from List B and circles it.

Step 3 Each player secretly estimates the other factor. Each player multiplies that factor by the circled factor.

The player whose product is closer to the circled target gets 1 point. If both players choose the same factor, then they each receive 1 point. The first player to reach 6 points wins. For each round players circle new numbers.

Use the Word!

Sometimes it is difficult to work with large numbers because they have so many digits. You can use place value and word form to help find products of some greater numbers.

Find 4 × 2,000,000.
Think: 4 × 2 million = 8 million.

So, 4 × 2,000,000 = 8,000,000.

Find 7 × 60,000.
Think: 7 × 60 thousand = 420 thousand.

So 7 × 60,000 = 420,000.

Use this strategy to find the products.

1. 7 × 1,000,000

   Think: 7 × 1 _____million_____ = _____7 million_____.

   So, 7 × 1,000,000 = _____7,000,000_____.

2. 8 × 10,000

   Think: ___8___ × ___10 thousand___ = ___80 thousand___.

   So, 8 × 10,000 = _____80,000_____.

3. 5 × 40,000

   Think: ___5___ × ___40 thousand___ = ___200 thousand___.

   So, 5 × 40,000 = _____200,000_____.

4. 9 × 30,000

   Think: ___9___ × ___30 thousand___ = ___270 thousand___.

   So, 9 × 30,000 = _____270,000_____.

5. 4 × 6,000,000

   Think: ___4___ × ___6 million___ = ___24 million___.

   So, 4 × 6,000,000 = _____24,000,000_____.

Name _____

Digit Detective

Complete the problem by finding the missing digits.

1.
```
      7 5
  ×   7 5
  -------
    3 7 5
  5,2 5 0
  5,6 2 5
```

2.
```
      3 2
  ×   4 7
  -------
    2 2 4
  1,2 8 0
  1,5 0 4
```

3.
```
      5 8
  ×   3 3
  -------
    1 7 4
  1,7 4 0
  1,9 1 4
```

4.
```
      6 4
  ×   2 4
  -------
    2 5 6
  1,2 8 0
  1,5 3 6
```

5.
```
      4 7
  ×   5 3
  -------
    1 4 1
  2,3 5 0
  2,4 9 1
```

6.
```
      5 4
  ×   3 6
  -------
    3 2 4
  1,6 2 0
  1,9 4 4
```

7.
```
      8 3
  ×   6 5
  -------
    4 1 5
  4,9 8 0
  5,3 9 5
```

8.
```
      7 3
  ×   5 4
  -------
    2 9 2
  3,6 5 0
  3,9 4 2
```

9.
```
      3 5
  ×   5 3
  -------
    1 0 5
  1,7 5 0
  1,8 5 5
```

10. Use the space below to create your own multiplication problems with missing digits. Ask a classmate to complete them. Check students' problems.

Name _____

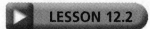

The Bigger, the Better

Players: 3 or more

Materials: Index cards numbered 1–9

Rules:

- One player draws six cards and pauses after each draw so that other players have time to decide where to write each digit.

- Players write the digits to make factors that give the greatest possible product. In every round, each player may throw out one digit.

- Once a player has written a digit, he or she cannot move the digit to another position.

- When the six cards have been drawn, players multiply to find their products. The player who has the greatest product wins the round. Answers will vary.

Number Thrown Out ↓

Number Thrown Out ↓

Round 1 ☐☐☐ X ☐☐ ○

Round 2 ☐☐☐ X ☐☐ ○

Round 3 ☐☐☐ X ☐☐ ○

Round 4 ☐☐☐ X ☐☐ ○

Round 5 ☐☐☐ X ☐☐ ○

Round 6 ☐☐☐ X ☐☐ ○

Lattice Multiplication

An early method of multiplying is the lattice method. Here's how it works.

Multiply 2,781 × 26.

- Write one factor along the top of the lattice and the other factor along the right side.

- Multiply each digit of the factors. Record the products inside the lattice so that the ones and tens are separated by a diagonal. (See Figure 1.)

- Add the numbers in the grid along the diagonals, starting from the lower right corner. Record each sum at the end of its diagonal—just as you do when adding columns. (See Figure 2.)

- Read the digits down the left and across the bottom. This is the product.

Figure 1

```
    2   7   8   1
  0/ 1/ 1/ 0/
0 / 4 / 4 / 6 / 2  2
  1/ 4/ 4/ 0/
1 / 2 / 2 / 8 / 6  6
```

So, 2,781 × 26 = 72,306.

Figure 2

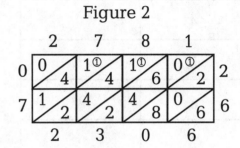

Use lattice grids to find the product.

1. 2,531 × 81 = _____ 205,011

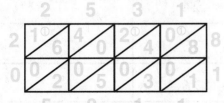

2. 6,491 × 34 = _____ 220,694

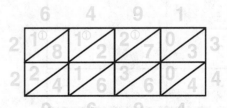

Doubling Tales

An ancient story tells of a clever traveling storyteller. He promised to entertain the king, and at a price that seemed unbeatable. For the first day the storyteller wanted only 1¢, and for each day after that the rate would double. The king thought about it briefly: 1¢ on day 1, 2¢ on day 2, and 4¢ on day 3. The king assumed that the price was reasonable.

How much will the storyteller charge the king on day 26?

Complete the table to find out.

Day	Price
1	1¢
2	2¢
3	4¢
4	8¢
5	16¢
6	32¢
7	64¢
8	$1.28
9	$2.56
10	$5.12
11	$10.24
12	$20.48
13	$40.96

Day	Price
14	$81.92
15	$163.84
16	$327.68
17	$655.36
18	$1,310.72
19	$2,621.44
20	$5,242.88
21	$10,485.76
22	$20,971.52
23	$41,943.04
24	$83,886.08
25	$167,772.16
26	$335,544.32

Do you think the storyteller charged a reasonable price? Explain.

Possible answer: No, he charged too much.

CW64 Challenge

Letter Go!

Each letter stands for a 1-digit number. Find a value for each letter.

1.
```
  AAA
+ BBB
-----
  CCC
```

There are 32
possible solutions.
Examples:

```
 111     222
+222    +111
----    ----
 333     333
```

2.
```
  MMM
  NNN
+ PPP
-----
  QQQ
```

There are 42
possible solutions.
Examples:

```
 111    111
 222    222
+333   +555
----   ----
 666    888
```

3.
```
  TTT
×   S
-----
  RRR
```

There are 4
possible solutions.

```
 333    444    222    222
×  2   ×  2   ×  3   ×  4
----   ----   ----   ----
 666    888    666    888
```

4.
```
   JJJ
×   KK
------
   JJJ
  JJJ
------
  JLLJ
```

There are 3
possible solutions.

```
  222      333      444
×  11    ×  11    ×  11
-----    -----    -----
  222      333      444
 2220     3330     4440
-----    -----    -----
2,442    3,663    4,884
```

5.
```
    EEE
×   FFF
-------
    EEE
   EEE
  EEE
-------
  EGHGE
```

There are 2
possible solutions.

```
    222       333
×   111     × 111
-------     -------
    222       333
   2220      3330
  22200     33300
-------     -------
 24,642    36,963
```

6.
```
   XX
×  YY
-----
   XX
  XX
-----
  XZX
```

There are 3
possible solutions.

```
   33      22      44
×  11    × 11    × 11
-----    ----    ----
   33      22      44
  330     220     440
-----    ----    ----
  363     242     484
```

Number Riddles

To solve the riddles on this page, you will need to know the name for each part of a division problem. Use the example at the right as a reminder.

$$\text{quotient} \longrightarrow 9 \text{ r}1 \longleftarrow \text{remainder}$$
$$\text{divisor} \nearrow 4\overline{)37} \longleftarrow \text{dividend}$$

1. My divisor is 5.
I am greater than 4 × 5.
I am less than 5 × 5.
My remainder is 1.

What dividend am I? __21__

2. My divisor is 9.
I am greater than 7 × 9.
I am less than 8 × 9.
My remainder is 7.

What dividend am I? __70__

3. My divisor is 8.
I am less than 30.
I am greater than 3 × 8.
My remainder is 5.

What dividend am I? __29__

4. My divisor is 6.
I am less than 60.
I am greater than 8 × 6.
I have no remainder.

What dividend am I? __54__

5. My dividend is 50.
My remainder is 1.
I am an odd number.

What divisor am I? __7__

6. My dividend is 8 times as large as my divisor.
I am an even number less than 15.

What quotient am I? __8__

7. My remainder is 8.
My dividend is 80.
I am a 1-digit number.

What divisor am I? __9__

8. My dividend is 24.
I am 2 more than my quotient.
I have no remainder.

What divisor am I? __6__

Complete to make a true equation. Possible answers are given.

9. (__5__ × __5__) + 2 = 27

10. (__3__ × __7__) + 5 = 26

11. (__7__ × __7__) + 3 = 52

12. (__5__ × __7__) + 1 = 36

13. Write your own number riddle below.

Check students' work.

_____

_____

CW66   Challenge

Name _____

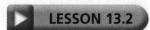
Cookie Coordinating

Joe and Melissa are organizing cookies to sell at a bake sale. They are making equal groups of each kind of cookie.

Complete the chart.

Total Number ÷ Number of Plates = Number of Cookies
on Each Plate

	Kind of Cookie	Total Number	Number of Plates	Number on Each Plate
	Chocolate chip	96	12 $12 \times 8 = 96$ $96 \div 12 = 8$	
1.	Oatmeal	42	14 $14 \times 3 = 42$ $42 \div 14 = 3$	
2.	Peanut butter	91	13 $13 \times 7 = 91$ $91 \div 13 = 7$	
3.	Butterscotch	76	19 $19 \times 4 = 76$ $76 \div 19 = 4$	
4.	Sugar	90	18 $18 \times 5 = 90$ $90 \div 18 = 5$	
5.	Ginger	36	12 $12 \times 3 = 36$ $36 \div 12 = 3$	

6. How many plates in all did Joe and Melissa use? _____ 88 plates

Challenge   CW67

Remainders Game

Number of players: 2, 3, or 4

Materials: game board
markers (24 small pieces of paper)
number cube labeled 3, 4, 5, 6, 7, and 8

Rules:

- Take turns placing a marker on one of the numbers on the board and rolling the number cube. Divide the numbers. For example, if you choose 92 on the board and roll a 3 on the number cube, you then write the problem $92 \div 3 = 30$ r2.

- Your score is equal to your remainder.

- After all the numbers on the board have been covered with markers, find the sum of your remainder scores. The winner is the player who has the greatest total score.

32	51	53	46	22	18
92	19	36	41	11	47
42	68	72	13	25	61
43	71	64	61	36	75

Name _____

Grouping Possibilities

Complete each table by finding different ways to divide a number into groups while always having the same remainder.

For example, $2\overline{)65}$ $= 32\,r1$ works in table 1,

but $3\overline{)65}$ $= 21\,r2$ does not work.

1.

Total	Number of Groups (less than 10)	Number in Each Group	Remainder
65	2	32	1
65	4	16	1
65	8	8	1

2.

Total	Number of Groups (less than 10)	Number in Each Group	Remainder
74	3	24	2
74	4	18	2
74	6	12	2
74	8	9	2
74	9	8	2

3.

Total	Number of Groups (less than 10)	Number in Each Group	Remainder
99	2	48	3
99	3	32	3
99	4	24	3
99	6	16	3
99	8	12	3

Riddle-Jam

Riddle: What do geese do in a traffic jam?

Find each quotient. Then write the quotients in order from least to greatest at the bottom of the page. Write the matching letter below each quotient.

1. $450 \div 5 =$ ___90___   Y   2. $270 \div 9 =$ ___30___   T

3. $3,600 \div 9 =$ ___400___   O   4. $42,000 \div 7 =$ ___6,000___   L

5. $2,100 \div 7 =$ ___300___   H   6. $7,200 \div 8 =$ ___900___   K

7. $36,000 \div 9 =$ ___4,000___   A   8. $280 \div 7 =$ ___40___   H

9. $3,500 \div 7 =$ ___500___   N   10. $240 \div 4 =$ ___60___   E

11. $56,000 \div 7 =$ ___8,000___   T   12. $49,000 \div 7 =$ ___7,000___   O

Riddle Answer:

30	40	60	90		300	400	500	900
T	H	E	Y		H	O	N	K

4,000		6,000	7,000	8,000
A		L	O	T	!

What's the Problem?

Write a problem that could be solved by using the division sentence. Then write a pair of compatible numbers, and estimate the quotient. Problems will vary. Accept reasonable estimates.

1. $1,489 \div 5 = n$

Problem: _____

_____

_____

_____

Compatible numbers:

_____ $1,500 \div 5 = 300$ _____

2. $7,100 \div 9 = n$

Problem: _____

_____

_____

_____

Compatible numbers:

_____ $7,200 \div 9 = 800$ _____

3. $63,147 \div 9 = n$

Problem: _____

_____

_____

_____

Compatible numbers:

_____ $63,000 \div 9 = 7,000$ _____

4. $276 \div 4 = n$

Problem: _____

_____

_____

_____

Compatible numbers:

_____ $280 \div 4 = 70$ _____

5. $758 \div 4 = n$

Problem: _____

_____

_____

_____

Compatible numbers:

_____ $800 \div 4 = 200$ _____

6. $41,797 \div 6 = n$

Problem: _____

_____

_____

_____

Compatible numbers:

_____ $42,000 \div 6 = 7,000$ _____

Break the Code

In the division problems below, each letter stands for a digit. The same letter stands for the same digit in all of the problems.

The table shows that H = 2 and T = 8. Use the division problems to find out what each of the other letters stands for.

0	1	2	3	4	5	6	7	8	9
A	L	H	R	D	E	I	F	T	W

Once you have broken the code, use the letters and digits to answer the riddle at the bottom of this page.

1.
$$\begin{array}{r} DD \quad\quad 44 \\ H)\overline{TT} \quad 2)\overline{88} \\ \underline{-8} \\ 08 \\ \underline{-\ 8} \\ 0 \end{array}$$

2.
$$\begin{array}{r} LH \quad\quad 12 \\ D)\overline{DT} \quad 4)\overline{48} \\ \underline{-4} \\ 08 \\ \underline{-\ 8} \\ 0 \end{array}$$

3.
$$\begin{array}{r} T \quad\quad 8 \\ I)\overline{DT} \quad 6)\overline{48} \\ \underline{-48} \\ 0 \end{array}$$

4.
$$\begin{array}{r} HT \quad\quad 28 \\ H)\overline{EI} \quad 2)\overline{56} \\ \underline{-4} \\ 16 \\ \underline{-16} \\ 0 \end{array}$$

5.
$$\begin{array}{r} T \quad\quad 8 \\ D)\overline{RH} \quad 4)\overline{32} \\ \underline{-32} \\ 0 \end{array}$$

6.
$$\begin{array}{r} LH \quad\quad 12 \\ E)\overline{IA} \quad 5)\overline{60} \\ \underline{-5} \\ 10 \\ \underline{-10} \\ 0 \end{array}$$

7.
$$\begin{array}{r} I\ rL \quad\quad 6\ r1 \\ F)\overline{DR} \quad 7)\overline{43} \\ \underline{-42} \\ 1 \end{array}$$

8.
$$\begin{array}{r} HH\ rH \quad\quad 22\ r2 \\ D)\overline{WA} \quad 4)\overline{90} \\ \underline{-8} \\ 10 \\ \underline{-\ 8} \\ 2 \end{array}$$

HOW DID THE RIVER HURT ITSELF?

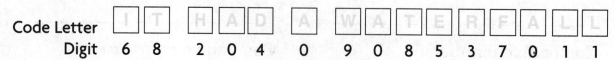

Code Letter	I	T		H	A	D		A		W	A	T	E	R	F	A	L	L
Digit	6	8		2	0	4		0		9	0	8	5	3	7	0	1	1

Remainders Game

Number of players: 2, 3, or 4

Materials: game board
markers (24 small pieces of paper)
number cube with the numbers 3, 4, 5, 6, 7, and 8

Rules:

- Take turns placing a marker on one of the numbers on the board and rolling the number cube. Divide the numbers. For example, if you choose 923 on the board and roll a 3 on the number cube, you then write the problem 923 ÷ 3 = 307 r2.

- Your score is equal to your remainder.

- After all the numbers on the board have been covered with markers, find the sum of your remainder scores. The winner is the player who has the greatest total score.

295	561	350	923	174	532
718	895	473	624	596	407
499	744	303	255	936	577
800	131	652	729	348	210

Answers will vary.

Super Checker!

Solve each division problem. Then complete the number sentence
that can be used to check the answer. Draw a line from the
division problem to the related number sentence.

1. $3\overline{)316}$ $\begin{array}{r} 105 \text{ r1} \\ \hline -3 \\ \hline 01 \\ -\ 0 \\ \hline 16 \\ -15 \\ \hline 1 \end{array}$

A.   (___5___ × 160) = ___800___

2. $5\overline{)800}$ $\begin{array}{r} 160 \\ \hline -5 \\ \hline 30 \\ -30 \\ \hline 00 \\ -\ 0 \\ \hline 0 \end{array}$

B.   (___3___ × 105) + 1 = ___316___

3. $4\overline{)831}$ $\begin{array}{r} 207 \text{ r3} \\ \hline -8 \\ \hline 03 \\ -\ 0 \\ \hline 31 \\ -28 \\ \hline 3 \end{array}$

C.   (___2___ × 309) + 1 = ___619___

4. $2\overline{)619}$ $\begin{array}{r} 309 \text{ r1} \\ \hline -6 \\ \hline 01 \\ -\ 0 \\ \hline 19 \\ -18 \\ \hline 1 \end{array}$

D.   (___7___ × 120) + 2 = ___842___

5. $7\overline{)842}$ $\begin{array}{r} 120 \text{ r2} \\ \hline -7 \\ \hline 14 \\ -14 \\ \hline 02 \\ -\ 0 \\ \hline 2 \end{array}$

E.   (___4___ × 207) + 3 = ___831___

Create a Problem

Write a word problem that could be solved with each division
sentence given. Then solve your creation! Problems will vary.

1. 237 ÷ 4 = _____ 59 r1

  Problem _____
  _____
  _____
  _____

2. 637 ÷ 6 = _____ 106 r1

  Problem _____
  _____
  _____
  _____

3. 4,822 ÷ 8 = _____ 602 r6

  Problem _____
  _____
  _____
  _____

4. 3,207 ÷ 9 = _____ 356 r3

  Problem _____
  _____
  _____
  _____

5. $97.35 ÷ 3 = _____ $32.45

  Problem _____
  _____
  _____
  _____

6. 2,517 ÷ 2 = _____ 1,258 r1

  Problem _____
  _____
  _____
  _____

Name _____

Diagram Division

Complete the division number sentence for each of the illustrations.

---

1.   Cookies

$$98 \div 4 = \underline{24} \ r\underline{2}$$

---

2.   Eggs

$$\underline{77} \div \underline{6} = 12 \ r5$$

---

3.   Marbles

$$145 \div 3 = \underline{48} \ r\underline{1}$$

---

4.   Crayons

$$\underline{182} \div \underline{5} = 36 \ r2$$

---

5.   Pennies in Piñatas

 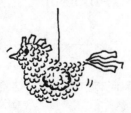 

$$\underline{\$9.87} \div \underline{3} = \$3.29$$

CW76   **Challenge**

Cookie Giveaway

You have 210 cookies to give equally to friends. There can be
no cookies left over. How many different groups can you make?

Write your groupings in the table. Fact families can help you.

Groupings Table		
210 ÷ 2 = 105 2 friends each get 105	210 ÷ 3 = 70 3 friends each get 70	210 ÷ 5 = 42 5 friends each get 42
210 ÷ 6 = 35 6 friends each get 35	210 ÷ 7 = 30 7 friends each get 30	210 ÷ 10 = 21 10 friends each get 21
210 ÷ 14 = 15 14 friends each get 15	210 ÷ 15 = 14 15 friends each get 14	210 ÷ 21 = 10 21 friends each get 10
210 ÷ 30 = 7 30 friends each get 7	210 ÷ 35 = 6 35 friends each get 6	210 ÷ 42 = 5 42 friends each get 5
210 ÷ 70 = 3 70 friends each get 3	210 ÷ 105 = 2 105 friends each get 2	210 ÷ 210 = 1 210 friends each get 1

Challenge CW77

Puzzled

Trace and cut out each of the figures below. See if you can build
an 8-by-8 square. Record your final square on the grid below.

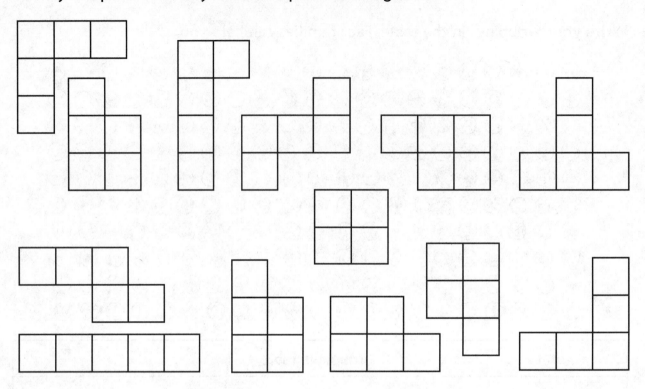

Possible solution:

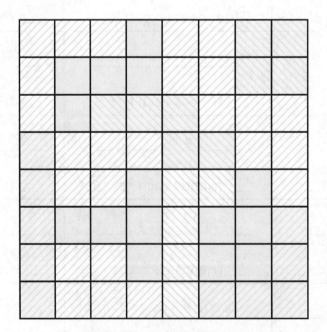

Name _____

Evenly Divided

How many ways can you divide a square into four equal pieces? Try to find at least six different ways. Solutions may vary. Possible solutions are shown.

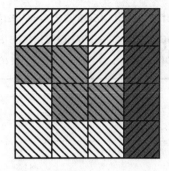

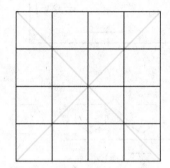
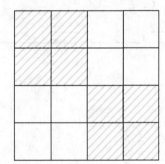

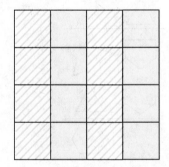
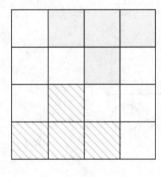

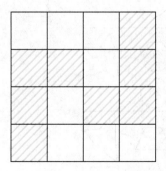
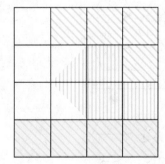

Division Cipher

Each shape in the exercises below represents a number 0–9.
Use your multiplication and division skills to find what number
each shape represents. Then fill in the key.

Key

1. ⏢ = 0, ⬟(pentagon) = 1, ◇ = 2, △ = 3, ⬡ = 4,

   _____   _____   _____   _____   _____

2. ▱ = 5, ☐ = 6, ☆ = 7, ⯃(octagon) = 8, ◯ = 9

   _____   _____   _____   _____   _____

Solve.

3.
  ◇2 △3
× ⬟ △3
─────────
  ☐6 ◯9
+ ◇2 △3 ⏢0
─────────────
  ◇2 ◯9 ◯9

4.

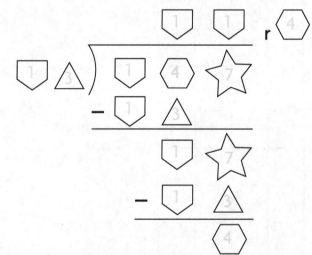

5.
    △3 ⬡4
  × ◇2 ▱5
  ─────────
  ⬟ ☆7 ⏢0
+ ☐6 ⯃8 △0
─────────────
  ⯃8 ▱5 ⏢0

6.

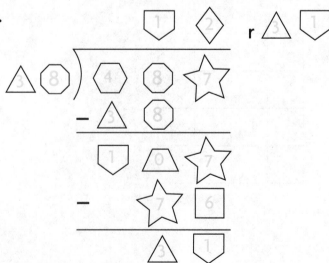

Name _____

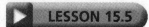

What's for Lunch?

Joe's Lunch Shop					
Hot dog	$1.09	Juice, small	$0.39	Cookie	$0.50
Hamburger	$1.59	Juice, medium	$0.59	Brownie	$0.75
Slice of pizza	$1.25	Juice, large	$0.69	Ice cream bar	$1.25

> Lunch Special $2.19
> Hamburger, medium juice, cookie

1. Lucas bought a hot dog, a large juice, and an ice cream bar. How much money did he spend on lunch?

   _____ $3.03 _____

2. Mr. Torres bought 4 lunch specials for his family. How much money did he spend?

   _____ $8.76 _____

3. Tom bought 2 hamburgers and a medium juice. What was his change from a $5 bill?

   _____ $1.23 _____

4. How much more does a hot dog, small juice, and a brownie cost than the lunch special?

   _____ $0.04 _____

5. In one week, the shop sold 246 hot dogs. The shop is open 6 days a week. What was the average number of hot dogs sold each day?

   _____ 41 hot dogs _____

6. On Monday, the cook made 6 whole pizzas. He cut each pizza into 8 slices. At the end of the day, there were 3 slices left over. How many slices of pizza did the shop sell that day?

   _____ 45 slices _____

7. During one week, the shop sold 272 slices of pizza. If each whole pizza is cut into 8 slices, how many whole pizzas did the shop sell during the week?

   _____ 34 pizzas _____

8. The shop sold 4 dozen brownies on Tuesday. How much money did the shop take in from brownie sales?

   _____ $36.00 _____

Name _____

Find the Missing Scores

Mr. Murphy gave his students 10 math quizzes last month. The highest possible score was 12 points.

A group of 3 students kept a record of their scores for the month.

1. Complete the chart by filling in the missing numbers.

	Hank	Sarah	Corina	Average Score on Each Quiz
Quiz 1	11 pts	12 pts	7 pts	10 pts
Quiz 2	10 pts	11 pts	6 pts	9 pts
Quiz 3	8 pts	7 pts	9 pts	8 pts
Quiz 4	9 pts	10 pts	8 pts	9 pts
Quiz 5	6 pts	6 pts	9 pts	7 pts
Quiz 6	12 pts	10 pts	11 pts	11 pts
Quiz 7	12 pts	9 pts	12 pts	11 pts
Quiz 8	9 pts	6 pts	6 pts	7 pts
Quiz 9	12 pts	11 pts	7 pts	10 pts
Quiz 10	11 pts	8 pts	5 pts	8 pts
Average Score for Each Student	10 pts	9 pts	8 pts	9 pts

2. Which student had the highest average score? _____Hank_____

3. For which quizzes were the average scores for the three students the highest?

_____Quiz 6 and Quiz 7_____

4. What is the difference between Sarah's average score and the group's lowest average score? _____2 pts_____

5. What does the number in the box at the lower right-hand corner of the chart represent?

_____Possible answers: the average of the group's score on_____

_____all the quizzes; the average of the individual_____

_____students' averages._____

CW82   Challenge

Divisible by 6

A number is divisible by 2 if the last digit of the number is even.
A number is divisible by 3 if the sum of the digits is divisible by 3.
A number is **divisible by 6** if it is divisible by 2 and by 3.

Example: 24 is divisible by 2 since 4 is even.
24 is divisible by 3 since $2 + 4 = 6$ and 6 is divisible by 3.
Since 24 is divisible by 2 and by 3, it is also divisible by 6.

Is the number divisible by 2, by 3, or by 6? Write **yes** or **no**.

1. 36   By 2? _yes_
         By 3? _yes_
         By 6? _yes_

2. 45   By 2? _no_
         By 3? _yes_
         By 6? _no_

3. 72   By 2? _yes_
         By 3? _yes_
         By 6? _yes_

4. 102   By 2? _yes_
         By 3? _yes_
         By 6? _yes_

5. 135   By 2? _no_
         By 3? _yes_
         By 6? _no_

6. 146   By 2? _yes_
         By 3? _no_
         By 6? _no_

7. 345   By 2? _no_
         By 3? _yes_
         By 6? _no_

8. 498   By 2? _yes_
         By 3? _yes_
         By 6? _yes_

9. 1,839   By 2? _no_
           By 3? _yes_
           By 6? _no_

10. 17,286   By 2? _yes_
             By 3? _yes_
             By 6? _yes_

Birthday Party Math

Shruti is planning a birthday party for her friends. For each situation, circle *Factor* if she should use factors to solve the problem or *Multiple* if she should use multiples.

1. Shruti is setting up tables for her guests. If there are 18 people coming, how many tables should she set, and how many people will be at each table?

   (Factor)   Multiple

2. Shruti's mother is buying forks for her guests to eat her cake. Forks come in boxes of 8. How many boxes of forks does Shruti's mother need to buy in order to have 16 forks?

   Factor   (Multiple)

3. Shruti is going to give away purple pencils as party favors. She has to order the pencils in sets of 10. How many sets of pencils should she order so that each guest can have two?

   Factor   (Multiple)

4. The guests will be playing some games. Shruti wants to form equal-sized teams. How can she form teams?

   (Factor)   Multiple

5. The guests are playing a game in a circle. They count off, starting with 1. Every 4th person wins a prize from the grab bag. Celia wants to know if she will win a prize. How can she figure out if she will win?

   Factor   (Multiple)

6. Shruti wants to write thank-you notes for her gifts. She wants to write the same number of notes each day. How many notes should she write each day?

   (Factor)   Multiple

Number Pyramids

The numbers in the pyramids are found by using one of these simple formulas:

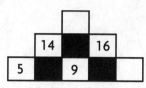

$A + B = C$ or $C - A = B$ or $C - B = A$

If you know some of the numbers, you can find the rest.

14	16
5	9

To find the top number, add. $14 + 16 = 30$

To find the lower number, subtract. $16 - 9 = 7$

Find the missing numbers in each pyramid.

1.

38
15 23
6   9   14

2.

26
17   9
10   7   2

3.

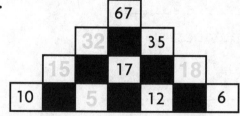

67
32   35
15   17   18
10   5   12   6

4.

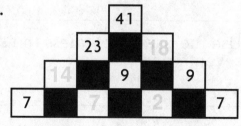

41
23   18
14   9   9
7   7   2   7

Now, make your own number pyramids. Exchange them with a partner, and test each other's math skills. Possible pyramid:

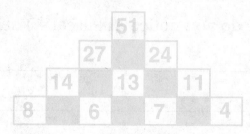

51
27   24
14   13   11
8   6   7   4

Pascal's Triangle

This triangle is called
Pascal's Triangle. To
get the next row of
numbers in the triangle,
add the two numbers
above.

```
              1
           1     1
         1    2    1
       1    3    3    1
     1    4    6    4    1
   1   5   10   10   5   1
```

The first row contains only one number, 1.

The second row contains 1 and 1.

1. Find the sum of the numbers in the third row. ____4____

2. Find the sum of the numbers in the fourth row. ____8____

3. Find the sum of the numbers in the fifth row. ____16____

4. Do you notice a pattern? What is it?

    Possible answer: Each row's sum is two times the

    sum from the previous row.

5. Use the pattern to guess the sum of the numbers in the
   seventh row.

    64

6. What are the numbers in the seventh row?

    1, 6, 15, 20, 15, 6, 1

7. What other patterns do you notice in Pascal's Triangle?

    Possible answers: Each row's number is the same as

    the number of terms in that row; there are diagonal

    patterns like 1, 2, 3, 4, 5, . . .; the first and last terms

    in each row are always 1.

Square and Not So Square Numbers

You know that 1 is a square number since $1 \times 1 = 1$.
You know that 4 is a square number since $2 \times 2 = 4$.
You also know that 9 is a square number since $3 \times 3 = 9$.

5, 6, 7, and 8 are not square numbers.
You cannot write any of these numbers as the product
of a whole number and itself.

For each list of numbers, tell which numbers are square numbers
and which numbers are not square numbers. The first one is done
for you.

1. 10, 11, 12, 13, 14, 15, 16, 17, 18, 19, 20, 21, 22, 23, 24, 25, 26

   Square: **16: $4 \times 4 = 16$; 25: $5 \times 5 = 25$**

   Not Square: **10, 11, 12, 13, 14, 15, 17, 18, 19, 20, 21, 22, 23, 24, 26**

2. 35, 36, 37, 38, 39, 45, 46, 47, 48, 49, 55, 56, 57, 58, 59

   Square: 36: $6 \times 6 = 36$; 49: $7 \times 7 = 49$

   Not Square: 35, 37, 38, 39, 45, 46, 47, 48, 55, 56, 57, 58, 59

3. 53, 54, 64, 65, 75, 76, 80, 81, 92, 93, 95, 100

   Square: 64: $8 \times 8 = 64$, 81: $9 \times 9 = 81$; 100: $10 \times 10 = 100$

   Not Square: 53, 54, 65, 75, 76, 80, 92, 93, 95

4. 110, 111, 115, 120, 121, 125, 140, 141, 142, 143, 144, 145

   Square: 121: $11 \times 11 = 121$; 144: $12 \times 12 = 144$

   Not Square: 110, 111, 115, 120, 125, 140, 141, 142, 143, 145

5. What are the 12 square numbers from the lists above.

   1, 4, 9, 16, 25, 36, 49, 64, 81, 100, 121, 144

Many Names

You can write many names for geometric figures from this line.

A — B — C (line with points A, B, C)

Points	Names for the Line	Names for the Line Segments	Names for the Rays
A, B, C	$\overleftrightarrow{AB}, \overleftrightarrow{BC}, \overleftrightarrow{AC},$ $\overleftrightarrow{BA}, \overleftrightarrow{CB}, \overleftrightarrow{CA}$	$\overline{AB}, \overline{BC}, \overline{AC},$ $\overline{BA}, \overline{CB}, \overline{CA}$	$\overrightarrow{AB}, \overrightarrow{BC}, \overrightarrow{AC},$ $\overrightarrow{BA}, \overrightarrow{CB}, \overrightarrow{CA}$

For 1–6, use the letters on the line below.

J — K — L (line with points J, K, L)

1. Write six different names for the line. 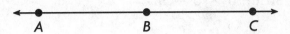 JK, KL, JL, LK, KJ, LJ

2. Name three different points. J, K, L

3. Write all the names for the different line segments.

    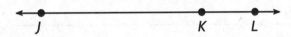 JK, KL, JL, LJ, LK, KJ

4. Show the three line segments marked on the line. Use a different color crayon for each line segment.

    J — K — L (line with points J, K, L)

    Name the line segment that goes with each color.

    Check students' work.

5. Write six names for rays.  JK, KL, JL, LJ, LK, KJ

6. Show three of the rays marked on the line. Use a different color crayon for each ray.

    J — K — L (line with points J, K, L)

    Name the ray that goes with each color.

     Check students' work.

Semaphore Code

The Semaphore Code was used by the United States Navy to send short-range messages. The message sender holds two flags in various positions to represent the letters of the alphabet.

To make a number, give the "numeral" sign first. Then use A = 1, B = 2, C = 3, and so on for the digits 1–9. Use J for zero.

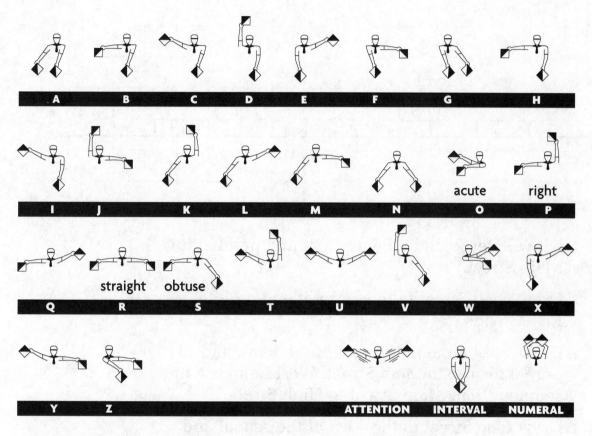

1. The Semaphore Code makes use of angles. Choose a letter and explain what kind of angle is shown.

_____ Answers will vary.

2. Write your name by using the Semaphore Code. For example, *Mark* would be   Check students' drawings.

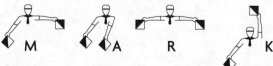

M   A   R   K

3. Now, write the year in Semaphore Code. Check students' drawings.

Name _____

Mapmaker, Mapmaker, Make Me a Map!

Use your knowledge of lines and angles and the following instructions to complete the map. Use a pencil and a ruler.

Check students' drawings. Possible drawing shown.

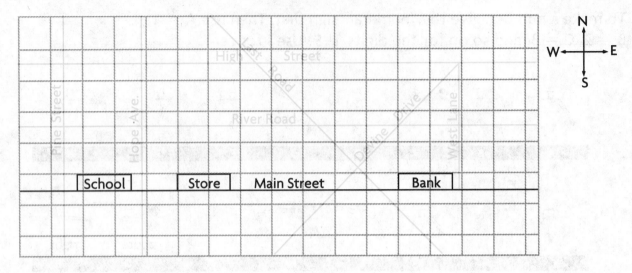

1. Draw River Road to the north of and parallel to Main Street.

2. Draw High Street to the north of and parallel to River Road.

3. Draw West Lane to the east of the bank and perpendicular to Main Street. West Lane is a line segment from Main Street to High Street.

4. Draw Pine Street to the west of the school and perpendicular to River Road.

5. Draw Hope Ave. to the east of the school and west of the store. Hope Ave. is parallel to West Lane.

6. Draw Devine Drive as a ray beginning at the intersection of West Lane and High Street. It moves southwest and intersects Main Street east of the store.

7. Draw Last Road perpendicular to Devine Drive, intersecting Main Street west of the bank.

Follow Their Paths

Use the grids and draw a diagram to solve. Be careful where you choose your starting point. Diagrams will vary.

1. Amy and Roger start at the same place. Amy walks 8 units east, 5 units south, and 3 units west. Roger walks 8 units east and 3 units south.

   Is Roger east or west of Amy? How many units?

   _____ east, 3 units _____

   Is Roger north or south of Amy? How many units?

   _____ north, 2 units _____

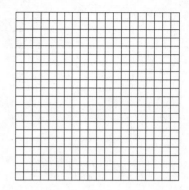

2. Shelly and Wade walk together south 6 units. Then Shelly walks 4 more units south and Wade walks 5 units east. Shelly walks 8 units west.

   Is Shelly east or west of Wade? How many units?

   _____ west, 13 units _____

   Is Shelly north or south of Wade? How many units?

   _____ south, 4 units _____

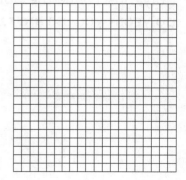

3. Brian and Arthur walk north together 4 units. Then Brian walks east 9 units and Arthur walks west 9 units. Brian and Arthur both walk south 3 units. Then Brian walks 5 units west.

   Is Brian north or south of Arthur? Explain.

   _____ Neither. Possible answer: They are both on _____

   _____ the same horizontal line. _____

   Suppose Arthur stays in the same place and Brian continues on to meet Arthur. How many units will Brian have walked in all?

   _____ 34 units _____

Polygon Figure

Use the numbers to name the polygons that make up the figure below. Write if any of the polygons are *regular*.

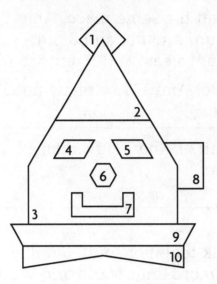

1. hexagon; 2. triangle, regular; 3. hexagon; 4. quadrilateral or parallelogram; 5. quadrilateral or parallelogram; 6. hexagon, regular; 7. octagon; 8. pentagon; 9. quadrilateral or trapezoid; 10. pentagon

Now draw your own polygon figure. Use at least three different polygons. Name the polygons that you use. Write if any of the polygons you use are *regular*.

Check students' drawings and answers. Answers should include at least three of the following shapes: triangles, quadrilaterals, pentagons, hexagons, and octagons.

Classify Triangles

1. How many different isosceles triangles can you find and name in the figure at right?

   4; △ABE, △CDE, △ADE, △BCE

   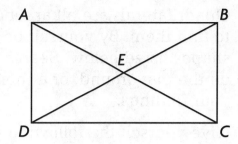

   equilateral triangles?

   0

   scalene triangles?

   4; △ABC, △ACD, △ABD, △BCD

   acute triangles?

   2; △AED, △BEC

   obtuse triangles?

   2; △ABE, △DEC

   right triangles?

   4; △ABC, △BCD, △CDA, △DAB

2. How many different isosceles triangles can you find and name in the figure at right?

   4; △ABD, △BDC, △ABC, △ADC

   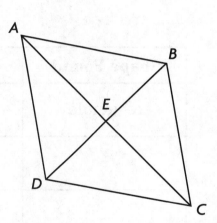

   equilateral triangles?

   0

   scalene triangles?

   4; △ABE, △ADE, △BCE, △CDE

   acute triangles?

   2; △ABD, △BCD

   obtuse triangles?

   2; △ACD, △ABC

   right triangles?

   4; △ABE, △BEC, △CED, △ADE

3. How many triangles are formed when any parallelogram and its diagonals are drawn?

   8

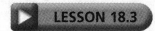

A Scavenger Hunt

Quadrilaterals are all around you. Here is your chance to find them. By yourself or in a small group, find the shapes listed below. Search for shapes in your classroom, on the playground, or at home. Use the chart to record your findings.

Give yourself the following points for each shape. Challenge yourself to find the harder shapes—and score more points!

Rectangle	1 point
Square	2 points
Rhombus	3 points
Trapezoid	4 points

Answers will vary.

Shape Found	Description	Points
rectangle	cafeteria table	1

Name _____

Diagram Detective

It is time for you to be a Diagram Detective. Look at the Venn diagrams in 1 and 2. Choose the labels that best describe each Venn diagram, and write them on the lines provided. You will not use all of the labels.

1. **A** ___Odd Numbers Between 0 and 20___

   B ___Multiples of 5 Between 0 and 28___

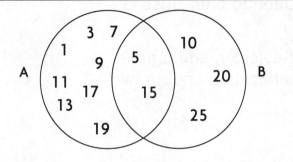

Venn Diagram Labels
Factors of 12
Odd Numbers Between 0 and 20
Even Numbers Between 0 and 20
Multiples of 3 Less Than 20
Multiples of 5 Between 0 and 28
Numbers Divisible by 2
Factors of 10

2. **A** ___Factors of 12___

   B ___Multiples of 3 Less Than 20___

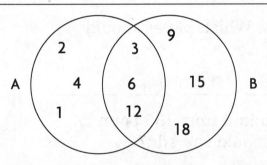

Think about how these months are related. Then write your own labels for the Venn diagram. Possible answers are given.

3. ___Months Beginning with a Vowel___

   ___Months Ending with R___

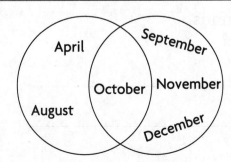

Circles

Help the athletes by choosing the correct plates to put on the weight-lifting dumbbell bar.

Remember the following:

- The dumbbell bar weighs 45 pounds.

- Plates weigh 5, 10, 25, 35, or 45 pounds.

- A matching plate must be added to both sides to balance the bar.

- It is quicker to use heavier plates. So, adding one 10-pound plate to a side is better than adding two 5-pound plates to a side.

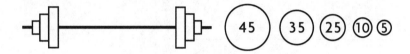

1. Anna wants to lift 135 pounds. Which plates should she use?

Possible answer: two 45-lb plates

2. Anna wants to increase the weight from 135 pounds to 185 pounds. Which plates should she add?

Possible answer: two 25-lb plates

3. The world record for weight-lifting is 765 pounds. Which plates would be needed for such a task?

Possible answer: sixteen 45-lb plates

4. Mark wants to lift about 300 pounds. What would you suggest he use?

Possible answer: six 45-lb plates

Name _____

Let It Snow!

Snowflakes are symmetrical ice crystals, showing both line symmetry and rotational symmetry. You can experiment with turns and with symmetry by making your own snowflakes.

a. Start with a square piece of paper.	**b.** Fold the square in half.	**c.** Fold in half again.
d. Fold in half again, along the diagonal.	**e.** Cut out various polygons to make a design.	**f.** Open the paper and find a symmetrical snowflake pattern.

1. Use square pieces of paper to cut out five different snowflakes.

2. Test each snowflake. Mark a central point in the middle of the snowflake.

3. Place the snowflake on a sheet of paper. Trace around the snowflake. Shade in the holes of the snowflake.

4. With your cutout snowflake lined up with your tracing, place a pencil on the central point. Rotate the snowflake 90°, 180°, 270°, and 360°.

Do your snowflakes have rotational symmetry? __yes__

Name _____

Similar Patterns

Trace each figure shown below. Then cut out figures to make pattern blocks.

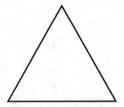  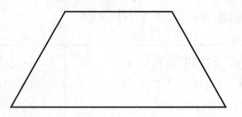

Are the pattern blocks that you made congruent to the original figures? Explain.

_____ Yes; they are the same size and same shape _____

_____ as the original figures. _____

Use each pattern block you cut out to draw at least one other figure that is similar but not congruent to the triangle, the square, and the pentagon. Check students' drawings. A sample of a similar figure is shown for each figure.

  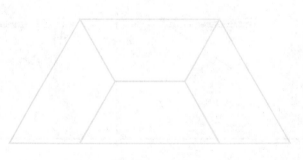

CW98 **Challenge**

Picture Perfect

Activity: Enlarge a picture.

Directions:

Step 1 Draw a square around
the figure you wish to enlarge.

Step 2 Use your ruler to draw a 1-cm grid
on your picture.

Step 3 Draw your figure on the grid
below. Since the grid you drew
on the picture is smaller than the
grid below, you will enlarge your picture.

Answers will vary.

Transforming Solid Figures

A **transformation** can be a **translation**, a **reflection**, or a **rotation**. A transformation does not change the original shape of the figure. So a figure that is translated, reflected, or rotated is still congruent to the original figure. Just as you can transform plane figures, you can transform solid figures.

Look at this rectangular prism:

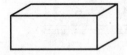

You can translate or reflect the prism to place the figure on this outline:	You can rotate the prism to place the figure on this outline:
⬜ (dashed rectangle)	⬜ (dashed square)

What transformation could you use to place the solid figure on the outline? Write *translation*, *reflection*, or *rotation*.

1.

   ___reflection___

2.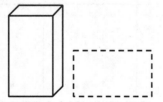

   ___rotation___

3.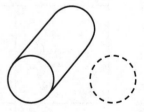

   ___translation___

Tell how many ways you can place the solid figure on the outline.

4.

   ___6___

5.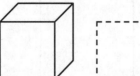

   ___24___

6.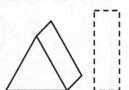

   ___6___

Name _____

Shapes in Motion

Here is your chance to practice translations, reflections, and rotations of a figure to make a tessellation.

Step 1 Read the numbers in the 4-by-4 grid.

Step 2 Replace the numbers with the matching symbols.

Step 3 Use two colors to help make the tessellation.

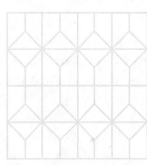

1	2	3	4
2	3	4	1
3	4	1	2
4	1	2	3

= 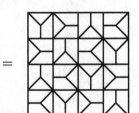 =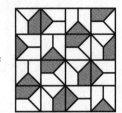

Complete, using the steps above. Designs will vary. Check students' work.

1.

3	3	3	3
1	1	1	1
3	3	3	3
1	1	1	1

 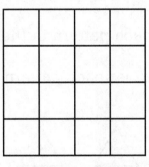

2.

1	3	3	1
4	2	4	2
3	1	1	3
1	3	3	1

=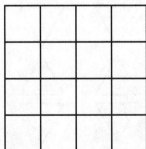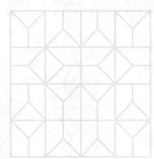

Use the puzzles above to help you make your own tessellation. Designs will vary. Check students' work.

3.

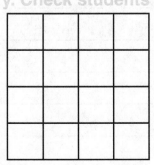 =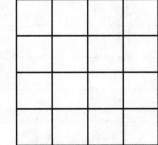

Name _____

Follow That Pattern

For 1 and 2, follow the rule and use the figure shown to create a pattern.

1. Rotate the oval 90° clockwise. Extend the pattern to show 8 figures.

2. Rotate the square 90° counterclockwise. Extend the pattern to show 7 figures.

3. Write a rule that describes each pattern in the first two rows of the pattern below.
Then, write a rule that describes each pattern in the first three columns.

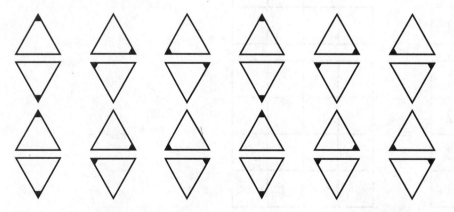

Rules: Sample answers are shown.

First row _____ Rotate the triangle one third turn clockwise. _____

Second row _____ Rotate the triangle one third turn counterclockwise. _____

First column _____ Reflect the triangle. _____

Second column _____ See below. _____

Third column _____ Reflect the triangle and then rotate one third turn clockwise. _____

Second column: Reflect the triangle and then rotate one third turn counterclockwise.

CW102 Challenge

Name _____

Fahrenheit Match-up

Match the temperature on the thermometer with the event by drawing a line to connect them.

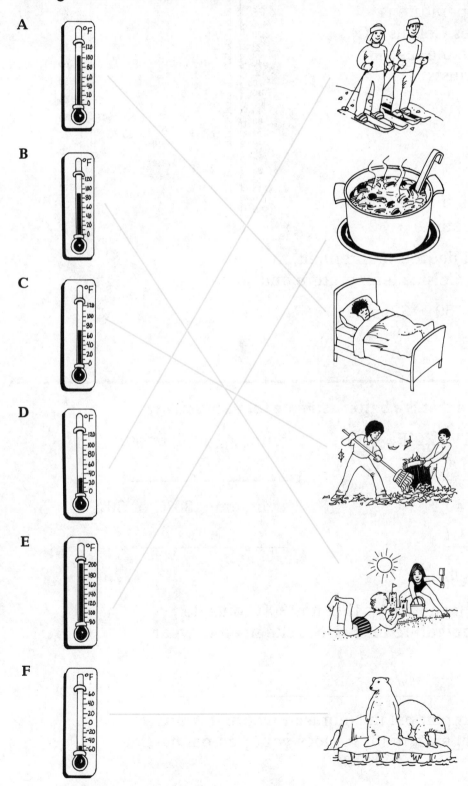

Heating Up

Temperature is measured in
degrees Fahrenheit (°F) in the
United States. Temperature is
measured in degrees Celsius (°C)
in countries that use the metric
system and by scientists.

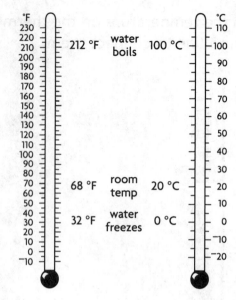

To estimate degrees °F, use this rule.
(2 × Celsius temperature) + 32 = ■ °F

To estimate 25°C in degrees Fahrenheit,
replace 25 with the Celsius temperature and solve.

(2 × 25) ⟶ 50 + 32 = 82

So, 25°C is about 82°F.

Write the temperature that is a better estimate for each activity.

1. ice hockey, 30°C or 30°F

   30°F

2. running, 50°C or 50°F

   50°F

3. surfing, 40°C or 40°F

   40°C

4. swimming, 30°C or 30°F

   30°C

For 5–6, use the rule above.

5. Your pen pal in Japan writes that it is 20°C outside.
   Estimate the temperature in °F. Does she need to wear a
   jacket?

   (2 × 20) + 32 = 72°F; probably doesn't need a jacket

6. You write to your pen pal in Nebraska where it is 9°C.
   Estimate the temperature in °F. Does your pen pal need a
   jacket?

   (2 × 9) + 32 = 50°F; probably needs a jacket

Number Riddles

Use a number line to help answer these number riddles.

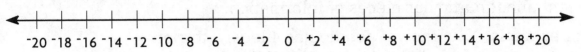

1. I am greater than +18 and less than +20. ____+19____

2. I am halfway between −2 and +8. ____+3____

3. I am between −10 and +4. I am 5 units away from 0.

   ____−5____

4. I am less than +5 and greater than −20. My two digits

   are the same. ____−11____

5. I am between −11 and +18. The sum of my digits is 5.

   ____+14____

6. I am between −20 and +20. My two digits read the
   same forward and backward. On the number line, I am

   to the left of 0. ____−11____

7. I am between −16 and +8. I am twice as far away from

   0 as 6 is. ____−12____

8. Make up your own number riddle. Give enough clues so
   there can be only one answer.

   ____Check students' work.____

   _____

   _____

Logical Conclusions

You use *inductive reasoning* when you make a general
statement about particular pieces of information.

> For example: You know a poodle has 4 legs, a terrier
> has 4 legs, a beagle has 4 legs, and a chihuahua has
> 4 legs. You use inductive reasoning to come to this
> conclusion: All dogs have 4 legs.

If you do not use enough information, you may *jump to a conclusion.*

> For example: Joy ate a steak that was tough. She used
> inductive reasoning to conclude that all steak is tough.
> Kent's steak was tender. He told Joy she jumped to the
> wrong conclusion.

You use *deductive reasoning* when you use a general
statement to draw a conclusion about a particular situation.

> Kayla learned all insects have 6 legs. She counts 8 legs on a spider.
> She comes to the conclusion that a spider is not an insect.

Write *inductive* or *deductive* to tell what kind of reasoning was
used to arrive at each conclusion. If the conclusion is incorrect,
write *jumped to a conclusion.*

1. Tyrone hears the bell chime once
   at 1:00, twice at 2:00, and 3 times
   at 3:00. He concludes the bell will
   chime the number of the hour.

   _____ inductive _____

2. In math Merri learned that the
   product of 0 and any number is
   always zero. She concludes the
   product of 234,687 and 0 is 0.

   _____ deductive _____

3. Ted looks at this pattern: 1, 4, 7,
   10, 13, ... He concludes that
   the rule for the pattern is + 3.

   _____ inductive _____

4. Ron wrote these multiples of 4:
   4, 8, 12, 16, 20, and 24. He
   concluded that the multiples
   of 4 are even numbers.

   _____ inductive _____

5. Jedd learned that prime numbers
   have only 2 factors: 1 and the
   number itself. He concluded that
   51 is a prime number.

   _____ deductive, jumped to conclusion _____

6. Lien read that a quadrilateral is
   a figure that has 4 sides. She
   concluded that a square is a
   quadrilateral.

   _____ deductive _____

Whole Number Puzzles

Example: I am a whole number.
   I am greater than 30 and less than 40.
   I am a multiple of 5.
   What number am I?

Graph the numbers greater than 30 and less than 40 on a
number line.

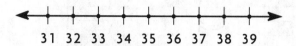

31 32 33 34 35 36 37 38 39

Which number is a multiple of 5? 35
The number is 35.

Use the clues to find each number. Graph numbers on a number
line to help you.

1. I am a whole number greater than 9 and less than 11.

   What number am I? __10__

2. I am a whole number. I am less than 20 and greater than 17.

   I am an even number. What number am I? __18__

3. I am a whole number. I am less than 9 and greater than 5.

   I am an odd number. What number am I? __7__

4. I am a whole number. I am greater than 10 and less than 14.

   I am an even number. What number am I? __12__

5. I am a whole number. I am greater than 15 and less than 20.

   I am a multiple of 3. What number am I? __18__

6. I am a whole number. I am greater than 10 and less than 16.

   I am divisible by 5. What number am I? __15__

7. I am a whole number. I am less than 20 and greater than 10.

   I am a multiple of both 3 and 4. What number am I? __12__

Checkmate!

Materials: colored pencils

The game of chess was invented more than 1,300 years ago. Today it is played in all parts of the world. Each piece has its own ways to move. For example:

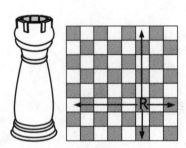

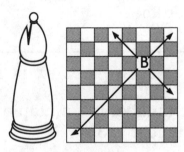

The *king* can move one square at a time. It can move up, down, left, right, or diagonally.

A *rook* can move up, down, left, or right. It can move any number of squares.

A *bishop* can move diagonally any number of squares.

For 1–4, use the drawing shown at the right.

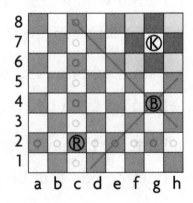

1. Which chess piece is in g4? ___bishop___

2. Which piece is in c2? ___rook___

3. Can the king move to h6? ___yes___

4. Can the bishop move to d8? ___no___

The queen is the most powerful chess piece. It can move any number of squares up, down, left, right, or diagonally. Suppose the queen is in b7. Can it move from b7 to each of the following squares? Write *yes* or *no.*

5. d7 ___yes___   6. d6 ___no___   7. a4 ___no___   8. g2 ___yes___

For Exercises 9–11, use colored pencils to color squares on the chess board. Check students' work.

9. Color blue all the squares to which the king can move. King's squares are shaded.

10. Color red all the squares to which the bishop can move. Bishop's squares have lines drawn through them.

11. Color yellow all the squares to which the rook can move. Rook's squares have small circles on them.

A Fraction of a Message

Decode the message. Find the fraction in the boxes below that
represents each letter on the number line. Write the letter of
that fraction in the message boxes.

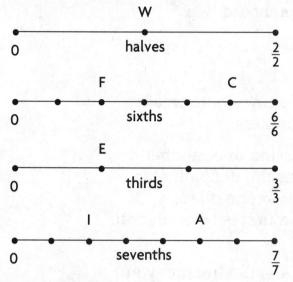

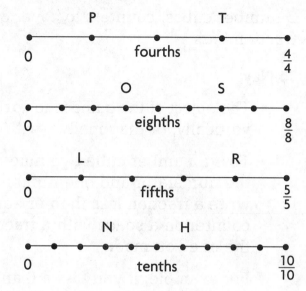

The message:

$\frac{5}{7}$
A

$\frac{2}{6}$	$\frac{4}{5}$	$\frac{5}{7}$	$\frac{5}{6}$	$\frac{3}{4}$	$\frac{2}{7}$	$\frac{3}{8}$	$\frac{3}{10}$
F	R	A	C	T	I	O	N

$\frac{2}{7}$	$\frac{6}{8}$
I	S

$\frac{5}{7}$
A

$\frac{1}{4}$	$\frac{5}{7}$	$\frac{4}{5}$	$\frac{3}{4}$
P	A	R	T

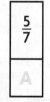

$\frac{3}{8}$	$\frac{2}{6}$
O	F

$\frac{5}{7}$
A

$\frac{1}{2}$	$\frac{6}{10}$	$\frac{3}{8}$	$\frac{1}{5}$	$\frac{1}{3}$
W	H	O	L	E

Make up your own coded message or riddle using the
number lines above. Add extra letters if you need them.

Answers will vary.

_____

_____

_____

_____

Equivalent Fraction Bingo!

Use your math skills with equivalent fractions to play bingo!

Materials:

2 number cubes, counters to cover gameboard,
fraction bars

To Play:

- The object of the game is to cover a row—horizontally,
vertically, or diagonally—with counters.

- Toss a number cube two times. Using one number as
the numerator and one number as the denominator,
write a fraction less than or equal to one. Place a
counter on a space with a fraction that is equivalent to
the one you made.

    For example, if you toss a 6 and a 4, the fraction you
    write is $\frac{4}{6}$. Look for an equivalent fraction such as $\frac{2}{3}$.
    Cover the space marked $\frac{2}{3}$ on the gameboard. (Use
    fraction bars to help find equivalent fractions.)

Gameboard

$\frac{2}{8}$	$\frac{4}{10}$	$\frac{6}{6}$	$\frac{2}{3}$	$\frac{1}{2}$
1	$\frac{2}{3}$	$\frac{2}{4}$	$\frac{6}{10}$	$\frac{8}{12}$
$\frac{6}{12}$	$\frac{1}{3}$	FREE	$\frac{1}{2}$	1
$\frac{1}{3}$	1	$\frac{1}{6}$	$\frac{1}{4}$	$\frac{2}{5}$
$\frac{1}{2}$	$\frac{2}{10}$	$\frac{2}{3}$	1	$\frac{1}{3}$

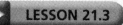

Estimating Fractional Parts

You can estimate the part of a whole that is shaded by thinking about benchmark fractions.

Example   About what part of this rectangle is shaded?
Is $\frac{1}{3}$ or $\frac{1}{2}$ the better estimate?

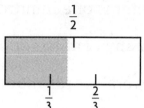

The part shaded is closer to $\frac{1}{2}$ than to $\frac{1}{3}$. So, $\frac{1}{2}$ is the better estimate.

What part of the figure is shaded?
Circle the fraction that is the closer estimate.

1.

$\frac{7}{8}$ or $\frac{3}{4}$

2.
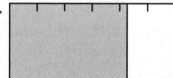

$\frac{2}{3}$ or $\frac{5}{6}$

3.
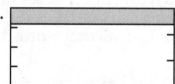

$\frac{1}{3}$ or $\frac{1}{4}$

4.
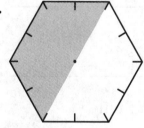

$\frac{4}{6}$ or $\frac{5}{12}$

5.
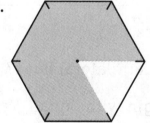

$\frac{2}{3}$ or $\frac{5}{6}$

6.
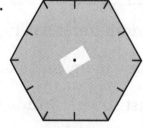

$\frac{2}{3}$ or $\frac{11}{12}$

7.
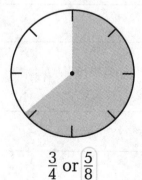

$\frac{3}{4}$ or $\frac{5}{8}$

8.
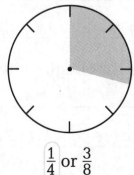

$\frac{1}{4}$ or $\frac{3}{8}$

9.
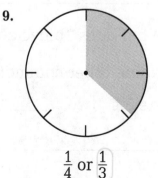

$\frac{1}{4}$ or $\frac{1}{3}$

Language Exploration

Use a dictionary to help you complete this page.

A **centi**meter is one hundredth of a meter or $\frac{1}{100}$ m.

1. How many centimeters are in a meter? _____ 100 centimeters _____

2. List several words that contain the root word "cent," and give
   their meanings. _____ Possible answers: century—100 years; _____

   centavo—means "hundredth" and is a Spanish coin;

   percent—one part of one hundred

A **tri**angle has three angles.

3. How many sides does a triangle have? _____ 3 sides _____

4. List several words that begin with "tri," and give their meanings.

   Possible answers: triathlon—a contest of 3 events: bicycling,

   running, and swimming; Triassic—the earliest of 3 parts of

   time used to measure geology; triad—a musical chord of 3 tones

A **quad**rilateral has four angles.

5. How many sides does a quadrilateral have? _____ 4 sides _____

6. List several words that begin with "quad," and give their
   meanings. _____ Possible answers: quadruple — four times as many; _____

   quadrant — a section on a grid that is divided into four sections

7. What does "bicycle" mean? _____ a vehicle with two wheels _____

8. Name other common words that begin with "bi," where "bi"
   means "two." _____ Possible answers: bicuspid—a tooth having _____

   two points; bifocal—eyeglasses with two-part lenses;

   bilingual—able to speak two languages

A Mixed-Number Challenge

Work together with a partner to write a mixed number that tells how much is shaded.

1.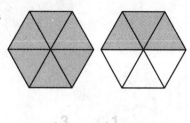

$1\frac{3}{6}$, or $1\frac{1}{2}$

2.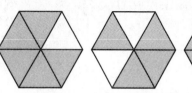

$2\frac{1}{6}$

Write a mixed number for each of the following figures. The figure at the right stands for 1.

3.

$1\frac{1}{6}$

4.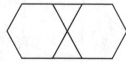

$2\frac{2}{6}$, or $2\frac{1}{3}$

5.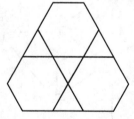

$3\frac{4}{6}$, or $3\frac{2}{3}$

6.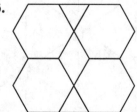

$4\frac{4}{6}$, or $4\frac{2}{3}$

7.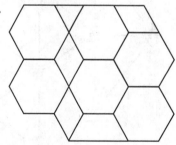

$7\frac{4}{6}$, or $7\frac{2}{3}$

Shade parts of the following figures. Have a partner write a mixed number that tells how much is shaded. Answers will vary.

8.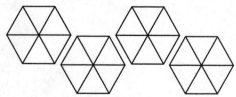

9.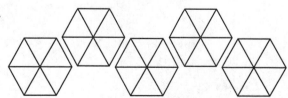

Amazing Maze

Find the path from the beginning to the end of the maze. Start with $\frac{1}{12}$ and add each fraction along your path. Your goal is to end at the finish with $6\frac{10}{12}$. Answers may vary.

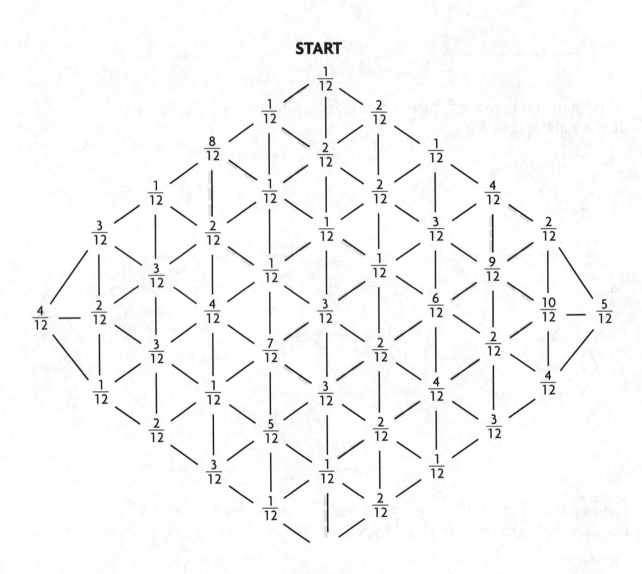

START

FINISH

Name _____

What's Left?

Color each picture as directed. Colors do not overlap.
When you are finished coloring, answer each question. Check students' coloring.

1. Color $\frac{1}{3}$ of the cake red.

   Color $\frac{1}{3}$ of the cake brown.

   How much of the cake is not

   colored? ___$\frac{1}{3}$___

   How much of the cake is

   colored? ___$\frac{2}{3}$___

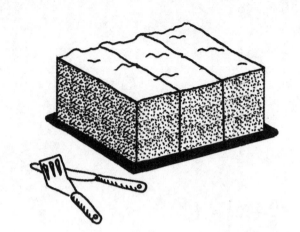

2. Color $\frac{6}{15}$ of the figure brown.

   Color $\frac{6}{15}$ of the figure orange.

   What fraction of the figure is

   not colored? ___$\frac{3}{15}$___

   What fraction of the figure is

   colored? ___$\frac{12}{15}$___

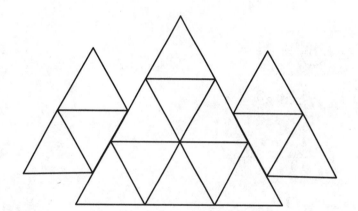

3. Color $\frac{8}{18}$ of the flag red.

   Color $\frac{2}{18}$ of the flag green.

   Color $\frac{2}{18}$ of the flag blue.

   Color $\frac{6}{18}$ of the flag orange.

   What fraction of the flag is not

   colored? ___$\frac{0}{18}$___

   What fraction of the flag is

   colored? ___$\frac{18}{18}$___

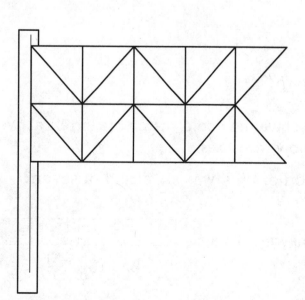

All Mixed Up!

Draw a line to connect the problem with the correct answer.

S. $5\frac{1}{8} + 3\frac{1}{8} = ?$ • $7\frac{3}{10}$

E. $6\frac{1}{3} + 5\frac{1}{3} = ?$ • 9

E. $10\frac{1}{2} - 1\frac{1}{2} = ?$ • $13\frac{5}{8}$

N. $4\frac{2}{5} + 3\frac{1}{5} = ?$ • $11\frac{1}{6}$

V. $15\frac{6}{8} - 2\frac{1}{8} = ?$ • $4\frac{1}{4}$

T. $10\frac{3}{4} - 6\frac{2}{4} = ?$ • $8\frac{1}{4}$

I. $8\frac{3}{7} + 2\frac{2}{7} = ?$ • $2\frac{2}{9}$

A. $7\frac{5}{6} - 6\frac{3}{6} = ?$ • $7\frac{3}{5}$

E. $5\frac{2}{10} + 2\frac{1}{10} = ?$ • $8\frac{1}{2}$

N. $10\frac{1}{12} + 1\frac{1}{12} = ?$ • $11\frac{2}{3}$

E. $6\frac{1}{4} + 2\frac{1}{4} = ?$ • $1\frac{1}{3}$

N. $10\frac{7}{9} - 8\frac{5}{9} = ?$ • $10\frac{5}{7}$

To solve the riddle, match the letters above with the answers below the boxes.

Riddle: Why was six afraid of seven?

Answer: because

$8\frac{1}{4}$ $8\frac{1}{2}$ $13\frac{5}{8}$ $7\frac{3}{10}$ $2\frac{2}{9}$ $1\frac{1}{3}$ $4\frac{1}{4}$ $11\frac{2}{3}$ $11\frac{1}{6}$ $10\frac{5}{7}$ $7\frac{3}{5}$ 9

What Breed Is Each Dog?

There are 48 dogs at the dog show.

Clue 1 Every dog is a specific breed.

Clue 2 The different breeds of dogs are: German shepherds, cairn terriers, poodles, golden retrievers, and Labradors.

Clue 3 Half of the dogs are German shepherds.

Clue 4 There are an equal number of cairn terriers and poodles.

Clue 5 There are twice as many cairn terriers as Labradors.

Clue 6 There are four golden retrievers.

1. List how many of each breed of dog there are.

   German shepherds = 24, cairn terriers = 8, poodles = 8,

   golden retrievers = 4, and Labradors = 4

2. What fraction of the group does each breed of dog represent?

   German shepherds = $\frac{1}{2}$; cairn terriers = $\frac{1}{6}$; poodles = $\frac{1}{6}$;

   golden retrievers = $\frac{1}{12}$; and Labradors = $\frac{1}{12}$

Name _____

Total Cost

Each coin of United States currency can be thought of as a fraction of a dollar.

One quarter is equal to $\frac{1}{4}$ dollar.

One dime is equal to $\frac{1}{10}$ dollar.

One nickel is equal to $\frac{1}{20}$ dollar.

One penny is equal to $\frac{1}{100}$ dollar.

1. Use coin values to help you find the sum. Use what you know about adding money to find the sum in simplest form.

Problem:	Think:	Steps:
$\frac{1}{4} + \frac{1}{10} = \frac{7}{20}$	One quarter + one dime $25¢ + 10¢ = 35¢$ $35¢ = \frac{35}{100} = \frac{7}{20}$	Write each coin as a fraction. Use what you know about money to write an equation. Write the sum in simplest form. So, $\frac{1}{4} + \frac{1}{10} = \frac{7}{20}$.

2. $\frac{1}{20} + \frac{1}{10} = \frac{3}{20}$

3. $\frac{1}{100} + \frac{1}{10} = \frac{11}{100}$

4. $\frac{3}{100} + \frac{4}{10} = \frac{43}{100}$

5. $\frac{2}{20} + \frac{3}{100} = \frac{13}{100}$

6. $\frac{1}{100} + \frac{6}{10} = \frac{61}{100}$

7. $\frac{3}{20} + \frac{4}{100} = \frac{19}{100}$

8. $\frac{1}{20} + \frac{2}{4} = \frac{11}{20}$

9. $\frac{31}{100} + \frac{4}{10} = \frac{71}{100}$

10. $\frac{6}{100} + \frac{41}{100} = \frac{47}{100}$

11. $\frac{19}{100} + \frac{12}{20} = \frac{79}{100}$

12. $\frac{1}{4} + \frac{6}{20} = \frac{11}{20}$

13. $\frac{5}{10} + \frac{3}{20} = \frac{13}{20}$

Cut Up!

You can subtract unlike fractions only after they have been renamed with like denominators.

Find $\frac{1}{2} - \frac{1}{4}$. $-$

$\frac{1}{2}$ $\frac{1}{4}$

Divide each half of the first figure in half. Both figures now have equal parts. Subtract the like fractions.

$\frac{2}{4}$ $\frac{1}{4}$ $\frac{1}{4}$

So, $\frac{1}{2} - \frac{1}{4} = \frac{1}{4}$.

For each pair of figures, find a way to divide one of them so that both have equal parts. Explain. Then subtract.

1.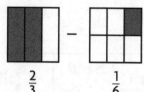

$\frac{2}{3}$ $\frac{1}{6}$

Divide the first figure in half
horizontally; $\frac{3}{6}$, or $\frac{1}{2}$.

2.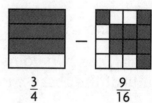

$\frac{3}{4}$ $\frac{9}{16}$

Divide the first figure vertically
in 4 equal parts; $\frac{3}{16}$.

3.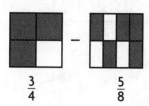

$\frac{3}{4}$ $\frac{5}{8}$

Divide both halves of the first
figure vertically; $\frac{1}{8}$.

4.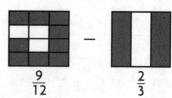

$\frac{9}{12}$ $\frac{2}{3}$

Divide the second figure horizontally into 4 equal parts; $\frac{1}{12}$.

Three Coins in a Fountain

When you toss a coin, there are just two possible outcomes: heads or tails.

If you toss two coins at once, there are three possible outcomes:

- 2 heads

- 1 head and 1 tail

- 2 tails

_____

For Problems 1–2, complete the sentence.

1. If you toss three coins at once, there are four possible outcomes: 3 heads, 2 heads and 1 tail,

   _____1 head and 2 tails,_____ and _____3 tails_____.

2. If you toss four coins at once, how many possible outcomes are there? What are they?

   _____5 possible outcomes; 4 heads, 3 heads and 1 tail,_____

   _____2 heads and 2 tails, 1 head and 3 tails, 4 tails_____

For Problems 3–4, use the table.

Try this experiment. Toss two coins at once, and tally the results of the tosses. Repeat for a total of 20 tosses.

2 Heads	1 Head and 1 Tail	2 Tails

3. Of the 20 tosses, how many times did you get 2 heads? 1 head and 1 tail? 2 tails?

   _____Answers will vary._____

4. Compare your results with those of your classmates. Which outcome seems more likely: 2 tails or 1 head and 1 tail?

   _____1 head and 1 tail_____

A Likely Story

A single dart can land anywhere on this dart board. The player's score is the number in the area the dart hits. Tell whether each event is *likely* or *unlikely*.

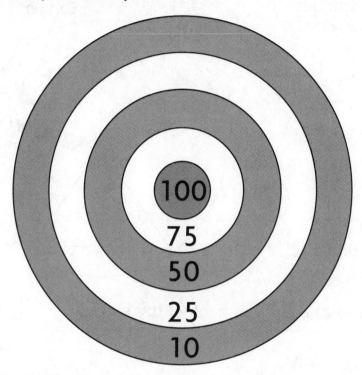

1. The score is an odd number. _____ unlikely _____

2. The score is an even number in a shaded section. _____ likely _____

3. The score is less than 100. _____ likely _____

4. The score is a number divisible by 50. _____ unlikely _____

5. The score is a number divisible by 10. _____ likely _____

6. The score is 25 or 50. _____ unlikely _____

7. The score is 10. _____ unlikely _____

8. The dart lands exactly in the center of the board. _____ unlikely _____

9. The dart lands in a shaded section. _____ likely _____

10. The dart lands in a section that is not shaded. _____ unlikely _____

Name _____

Certainly Not!

Remember, if an event is *certain*, it will always happen. If
an event is *impossible*, it will never happen.

1. Write numbers in the spinner
so that each of the following
events is certain.

   The pointer stopping on a
   number

   A. that is greater than 25

   B. that has 12 as a factor

   C. that is divisible by 3

   D. that has the sum of 8 or
   more when its two digits
   are added together

A possible answer is given.

Certain

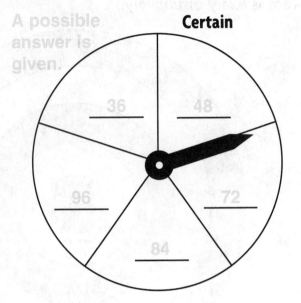

36   48

96   72

84

2. Write numbers in the spinner so that each of the events
above is impossible. A possible answer is given.

Impossible

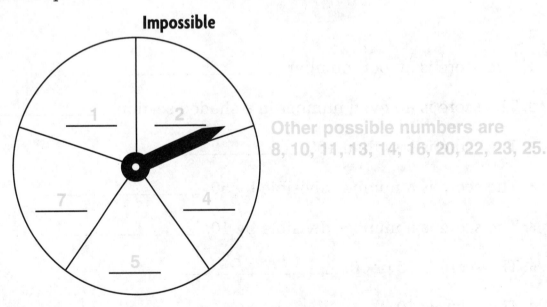

1   2

7   4

5

Other possible numbers are
8, 10, 11, 13, 14, 16, 20, 22, 23, 25.

3. Look at the spinner in Problem 2. Write two more events
that would be impossible if you were to use the spinner.

   Answers may vary.

   _____

   _____

Heads or Tails?

A coin should land on heads about half of the time.

What if you toss a coin 10 times? Are you likely to get 5 heads and 5 tails?

What if you toss a coin 50 times? Are you likely to get 25 heads and 25 tails?

Try these experiments before you answer.

1. Toss a coin 10 times. Record your tallies in the table. Check students' tables.

2. Toss a coin 50 times. Record your tallies in the table. Check students' tables.

Heads	Tails	Total
		10
		50

3. Compare your results with those of your classmates. How many students got exactly 5 heads and 5 tails? How many students got exactly 25 heads and 25 tails?

_____ Answers will vary. _____

4. Find the fraction (in simplest form) of heads for both experiments, as follows. Possible answers are given.

Experiment 1: $\dfrac{\text{number of heads}}{10} = \dfrac{2}{5}$

Experiment 2: $\dfrac{\text{number of heads}}{50} = \dfrac{27}{50}$

Compare the fractions in Problem 4 with those of your classmates. Then complete 5–7. Write *likely* or *unlikely*.

5. If you toss a coin 10 times, you are ____unlikely____ to get exactly 10 heads.

6. If you toss a coin 50 times, you are ____unlikely____ to get exactly 50 heads.

7. If you toss a coin 50 times, you are ____likely____ to get between 20 and 30 heads.

Name _____

The Path of Probability

Toss a coin 5 times to follow a probability path from the start to the end boxes.

Rules **a.** Toss the coin. If it is heads, follow the heads path to the next oval. If it is tails, follow the tails path.

b. Put a tally mark in an oval for each toss.

c. After 5 tosses, record the letter of the box in which you land.

d. Repeat the process 20 times.

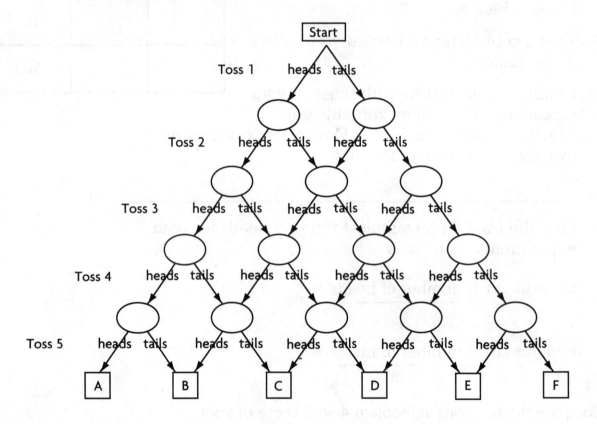

1. In which lettered boxes did you finish most often?

   Possible answer: C and D

   _____

2. In which boxes did you finish least often?

   Possible answer: A and F

   _____

Name _____

Mystery Cube

Yancy wrote 6 different one-digit numbers on a cube. Then he made an identical cube. The line plot shows the sums and the number of ways he could get each sum if he were to toss his two number cubes.

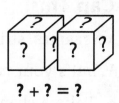

? + ? = ?

```
              X
          X   X   X
        X   X   X   X
      X   X   X   X   X   X
    X   X   X   X   X   X   X
  X   X   X   X   X   X   X   X   X
  +---+---+---+---+---+---+---+---+---+---+---+---+---+---+
  5   6   7   8   9  10  11 12 13 14 15 16 17 18 19
```
Sums

HINT: If Yancy wrote the numbers 4 and 5 on each cube, he would count getting 4 + 5 and 5 + 4 as two different ways to toss.

Answer the question.

1. If 1 were the least number on each cube, what would be the least sum that could be marked on a line plot? __2__

Use the line plot. Complete the table below to find the 6 one-digit numbers Yancy wrote on each cube.

2.

Sum	Number of Ways to Toss	Ways to Toss the Sum
8	1	4 + 4
9	2	4 + 5, 5 + 4
10	3	4 + 6, 6 + 4, 5 + 5
11	4	4 + 7, 7 + 4, 5 + 6, 6 + 5
12	5	4 + 8, 8 + 4, 5 + 7, 7 + 5, 6 + 6
13	6	4 + 9, 9 + 4, 5 + 8, 8 + 5, 6 + 7, 7 + 6
14	5	5 + 9, 9 + 5, 6 + 8, 8 + 6, 7 + 7
15	4	6 + 9, 9 + 6, 7 + 8, 8 + 7
16	3	7 + 9, 9 + 7, 8 + 8
17	2	8 + 9, 9 + 8
18	1	9 + 9

3. The numbers Yancy wrote on each cube are _____4, 5, 6, 7, 8, 9_____.

Name _____

Cap This!

MATERIALS string 24 inches long, customary ruler

What's your cap size?

• Take a string and carefully measure around your head.

• Mark the string, and then lay it down along a ruler. Read the measure to the nearest half inch.

• Record your cap size.

• Take a survey to find the cap size of ten of your classmates.

Name	Cap Size

What is the average cap size for the ten classmates in your survey? Explain.

Answers will vary.

_____

_____

_____

_____

_____

Path Finder

1. Measure every path to the nearest inch or half inch.
Write the length on the path.

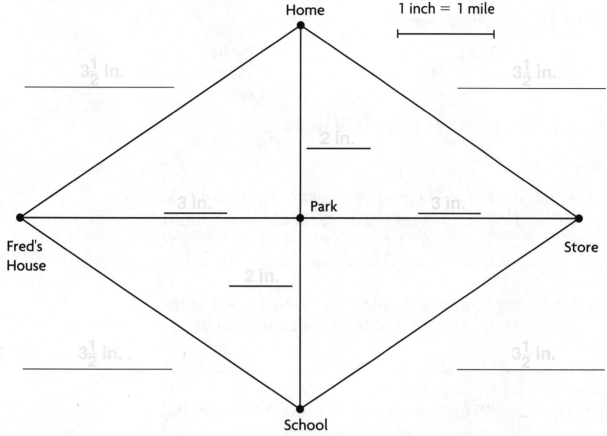

Home

1 inch = 1 mile

$3\frac{1}{2}$ in. _____

$3\frac{1}{2}$ in. _____

2 in. _____

3 in. _____   Park   3 in. _____

Fred's
House

Store

2 in. _____

$3\frac{1}{2}$ in. _____

$3\frac{1}{2}$ in. _____

School

2. List four ways to drive from home to school, following
these guidelines. Always travel down and to the right or
left. Do not retrace your path. Possible answers:
home – Fred's – school; home – Fred's – park – school;
home – Fred's – park – store – school; home – park – Fred's – school;
home – park – store – school; home – park – school; home – store –
school; home – store – park – school; home – store – park – Fred's – school

_____

_____

3. What is the longest route? How many miles is it?
home – Fred's – park – store – school, or home – store – park –
Fred's – school; 13 mi

_____

4. What is the shortest route? How many miles is it?

home – park – school; 4 mi

_____

5. About how long would it take you to walk the shortest route

to school? HINT: It takes about 20 minutes to walk a mile. _____ about 80 min

Challenge   CW127

Cut the Measure

You have 2 feet of ribbon. You need 20 inches of the ribbon. How many inches of ribbon should you cut off?

Find the equivalent measure.　　　Subtract.

1 foot = 12 inches
2 feet = 2 × 12, or 24 inches

$$\begin{array}{r} 24 \text{ inches} \\ - \ 20 \text{ inches} \\ \hline 4 \text{ inches} \end{array}$$

So, you should cut off 4 inches of ribbon.

Solve.

1. You have 8 feet of string. You need 2 yards of the string. How many feet of string should you cut off?

_____ 2 ft

2. You have 6 yards of fabric. You need 14 feet of the fabric. How many feet of fabric should you cut off?

_____ 4 ft

3. You have 38 inches of cord. You need 3 feet of the cord. How many inches of cord should you cut off?

_____ 2 in.

4. You have 4 feet of lace. You need 45 inches of the lace. How many inches of lace should you cut off?

_____ 3 in.

5. You have 2 yards of wrapping paper. You need 65 inches of the paper. How many inches of paper should you cut off?

_____ 7 in.

Half Full or Half Empty?

The pitchers below are the same size. They are arranged from barely full to completely full. Each pitcher can be labeled with two equal measurements. Use the measures in the box to write in the missing measurement for each pitcher.

> 8 cups, 3 quarts, 4 quarts,
> 6 pints, 1 gallon, 1 quart, 6 cups

1.

1 pint or 2 cups

2.

2 pints or _____1 quart_____

3.

3 pints or _____6 cups_____

4.

4 pints or _____8 cups_____

5.

_____6 pints_____ or _____3 quarts_____

6.

_____1 gallon_____ or _____4 quarts_____

Which Weight?

The weights below belong on the balances. Some of the balances are unbalanced. Match each weight listed below with one of the problems to make a true statement. Use each weight once.

16 ounces, 32 ounces, 48 ounces, 52 ounces, 96 ounces, 5 pounds, 4,000 pounds, 8 tons

1.
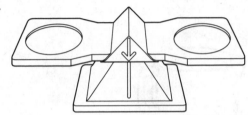

2 pounds = ___32 ounces___

2.
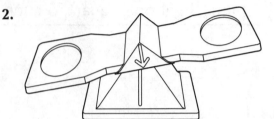

24 ounces > ___16 ounces___

3.
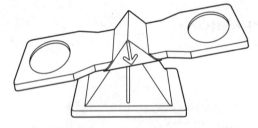

4 pounds > ___52 ounces___

4.
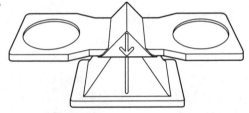

2 tons = ___4,000 pounds___

5.
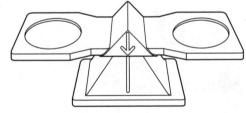

6 pounds = ___96 ounces___

6.
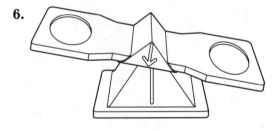

6 tons < ___8 tons___

7.
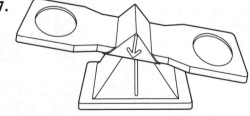

24 ounces < ___5 pounds___

8.
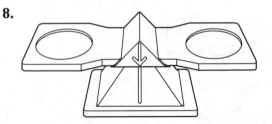

3 pounds = ___48 ounces___

Name _____

Atlas Stones

At the annual "World's Strongest Person" competition, no event tests athletic strength better than the Stones of Atlas. Competitors must lift six progressively larger round stones onto 3-foot platforms. The stones are huge—about 2–3 feet in diameter. Their weight is staggering.

The weight of the Stones of Atlas is given in the ancient measurement of *stones*. A stone is about 14 pounds.

Convert the weight of the 6 Atlas Stones into pounds.

1. 10 stones ≈ _____140_____ lb

2. 13 stones ≈ _____182_____ lb

3. 15 stones ≈ _____210_____ lb

4. 18 stones ≈ _____252_____ lb

5. 20 stones ≈ _____280_____ lb

6. 23 stones ≈ _____322_____ lb

7. In the 1995 event, one competitor executed a dead lift of 952 pounds. How many stones would that be?

_____ about 68 stones _____

8. Some of the competitors in the "World's Strongest Person" competition weigh 30 stones. What is their weight in pounds?

_____ about 420 lb _____

9. Figure out how much the following people in Doreen's family weigh in stones. Complete the chart. Round to the nearest whole number.

Name	Weight in Pounds	Weight in Stones
Doreen	76	5
Natalie	92	7
Jake	105	8
Mrs. Snell	146	10
Mr. Snell	207	15

Point A to Point B

1. Measure and record the length of each line to the nearest centimeter. Then record the length in decimeters.

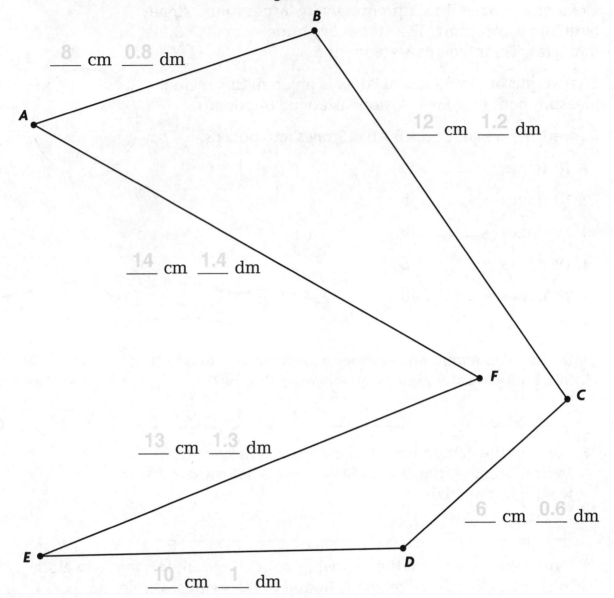

_8_ cm _0.8_ dm

_12_ cm _1.2_ dm

_14_ cm _1.4_ dm

_13_ cm _1.3_ dm

_6_ cm _0.6_ dm

_10_ cm _1_ dm

2. Start at *A* and measure clockwise until you are back at *A*.

 a. How many centimeters is this measure? _63 cm_

 b. How many decimeters is this measure? _6.3 dm_

 c. How many times would you need to measure around this figure to have a measure of 5 meters? _8 times_

CW132 Challenge

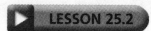

Wedding Fun

Sam and Sarah are getting married. Their friends are tying cans to the back of their car. How many meters long is the rope they are using?

To find out:

- Place the measurements in order from least to greatest in the cake.

- Complete the squares from left to right and from bottom to top.

- Add the measurements in the starred boxes to find how long the rope is.

_____ The rope is 3 m long.

> 7 dm, 250 cm, 1 m, 5 cm, 6 dm,
> 1 dm, 180 cm, 14 dm, 280 mm,
> 20 dm, 88 cm, 32 cm, 3 dm,
> 120 cm, 15 cm, 210 cm, 2 cm,
> 9 dm, 10 mm, 215 cm, 48 cm

250 cm					
★ 210 cm	215 cm				
14 dm	180 cm	20 dm			
88 cm	★ 9 dm	1 m	120 cm		
3 dm	32 cm	48 cm	6 dm	7 dm	
10 mm	2 cm	5 cm	1 dm	15 cm	280 mm

Just Married

Name _____

Punch All Around

> **Fruity-Tutty Punch Recipe**
>
> 1 liter orange juice
> 250 milliliters pineapple juice
> 500 milliliters apple juice
> 100 milliliters kiwi juice
> 50 milliliters lemon juice
> 2 liters seltzer water

1. List the recipe ingredients from the least to the greatest amount.

lemon juice, kiwi juice, pineapple juice, apple juice,

orange juice, seltzer water

2. How much punch will the recipe make in milliliters?

_____ 3,900 mL _____

3. A punch glass holds about 300 mL. About how many

glasses does the recipe make? _____ about 13 glasses _____

4. You sell a glass of punch for $0.50. About how much
money will you take in if you sell all the punch one

recipe makes? _____ about $6.50 _____

5. It costs $4.87 for all the punch ingredients. About how

much money will you make? _____ about $1.63 _____

6. Your punch is so popular, you are asked to make
enough for 100 glasses. About how many times will

you need to make the recipe? _____ about 8 times _____

7. You charge $0.75 a glass. How much money will

you take in? _____ $75.00 _____

8. Your cost for all the ingredients is $38.96. How

much money will you make? _____ $36.04 _____

CW134 Challenge

Name _____

Sweet Enough

How many sugar packs would it take to balance each mass?

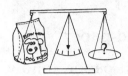

1.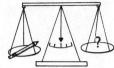

1 gram = ___1 sugar pack___

2.

2 kg = ___2,000 sugar packs___

3.

80 kg = ___80,000 sugar packs___

4.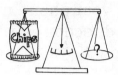

25 g = ___25 sugar packs___

Write the mass in grams and kilograms.

5. 4,000 sugar packs = ___4,000 g and 4 kg___

6. 6,000 sugar packs = ___6,000 g and 6 kg___

7. 2,000 sugar packs = ___2,000 g and 2 kg___

8. 1,000 sugar packs = ___1,000 g and 1 kg___

9. 3,000 sugar packs = ___3,000 g and 3 kg___

10. 5,000 sugar packs = ___5,000 g and 5 kg___

Find the number of sugar packs in each box.

11.  **SUGAR** 25 kg

___25,000 sugar packs___

12.  **SUGAR** 16 kg

___16,000 sugar packs___

13. 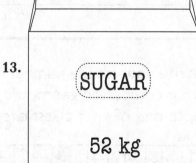 **SUGAR** 52 kg

___52,000 sugar packs___

Ring-A-Ling

When you graph your phone number, does it make a geometric pattern?

YOU WILL NEED grid paper

On a piece of grid paper, follow these directions.

• Start in the center of the grid paper.

• Use the digits in your phone number to decide how far to move in each direction. Write your phone number four times in a row.

• Move up (↑), then right (→), then down (↓), then left (←). Continue this process until there are no more digits.

For example:

The phone number 321-4123 would make the following moves:

• 3 up, 2 right, 1 down, 4 left, 1 up, 2 right, 3 down, 3 left, and so on.

• The result is the figure at the right.

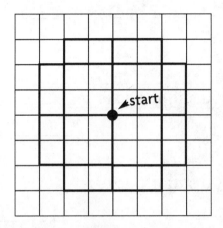

Write your phone number 4 times. Graph your numbers. Compare your completed geometric pattern with the one shown above and with one of your classmates'. Check students' graphs.

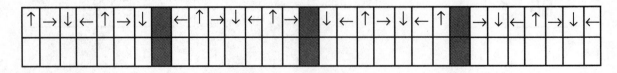

CW136 Challenge

Measurement Sense

1. The punch bowl holds 2 liters of punch. About how many pints of punch does the punch bowl hold? Explain.

   Sample answer: about 4 pt: 4 pt = 2 qt and 2 qt ≈ 2 L

2. Marisa runs in a 10-kilometer race. About how many miles long is the race? Explain.

   Sample answer: about 6 mi: 1 kilometer is a little

   longer than $\frac{1}{2}$ mile, so the race is a little longer

   than half of 10 miles, or about 6 mi.

3. A container holds 180 grams of yogurt. About how many ounces of yogurt are in the container? Explain.

   Sample answer: about 6 oz, since 1 oz ≈ 30 g

4. Joshua walked around the path 3 times. The path is 1,500 meters long. Did he walk more than 2 miles? Explain.

   Yes. Sample answer: 1 mi ≈ 1,600 m, so

   2 mi ≈ 3,200 m; Joshua walked 1,500 m × 3,

   or 4,500 m, and 4,500 m > 3,200 m

5. A bottle holds 12 ounces of juice. About how many grams of juice are in the bottle? Explain.

   Sample answer: about 336 g: 1 oz ≈ 28 g and

   28 × 12 = 336

6. A bag of potatoes weighs 5 pounds. Estimate the mass of the bag of potatoes in kilograms. Is your estimate greater than or less than the exact mass? Explain.

   Sample answer: about $2\frac{1}{2}$ kg: 1 kilogram is

   a little more than 2 pounds, so the estimate

   is greater than the exact mass.

Riddlegram!

Answer this riddle. Write the letter that matches each fraction or decimal.
You will use some models more than once.

Riddle: What did one Math book say to the other Math book?

$\underset{0.2}{\underline{\text{B}}}$ $\underset{0.6}{\underline{\text{O}}}$ $\underset{\frac{5}{10}}{\underline{\text{Y}}}$, $\underset{\frac{8}{10}}{\underline{\text{D}}}$ $\underset{\frac{6}{10}}{\underline{\text{O}}}$ $\underset{0.01}{\underline{\text{I}}}$ $\underset{\frac{49}{100}}{\underline{\text{H}}}$ $\underset{0.52}{\underline{\text{A}}}$ $\underset{0.9}{\underline{\text{V}}}$ $\underset{0.35}{\underline{\text{E}}}$

$\underset{0.3}{\underline{\text{P}}}$ $\underset{\frac{1}{10}}{\underline{\text{R}}}$ $\underset{0.6}{\underline{\text{O}}}$ $\underset{\frac{2}{10}}{\underline{\text{B}}}$ $\underset{0.12}{\underline{\text{L}}}$ $\underset{\frac{35}{100}}{\underline{\text{E}}}$ $\underset{0.7}{\underline{\text{M}}}$ $\underset{\frac{15}{100}}{\underline{\text{S}}}$!

B
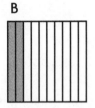

Y
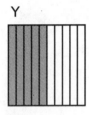

S
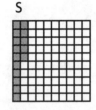

V
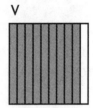

H
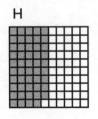

P
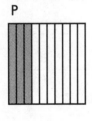

A
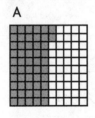

D
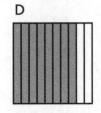

L
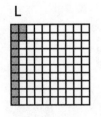

M
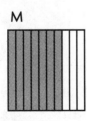

R

E
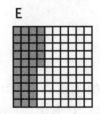

O
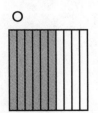

I
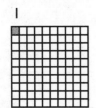

Name _____

Ten-Thousandths

You can extend the place-value chart to show the
next place value after thousandths.

Ones	.	Tenths	Hundredths	Thousandths	Ten-Thousandths
0	.	0	0	0	6
0	.	0	0	2	6
0	.	0	3	2	6
0	.	5	3	2	6

Standard Form		**Word Form**
0.0006	→	six ten-thousandths
0.0026	→	twenty-six ten-thousandths
0.0326	→	three hundred twenty-six ten-thousandths
0.5326	→	five thousand three hundred twenty-six ten-thousandths

Write each number in word form.

1. 0.0008 _____eight ten-thousandths_____

2. 0.0079 _____seventy-nine ten-thousandths_____

3. 0.0965 _____nine hundred sixty-five ten-thousandths_____

4. 0.2346 _____two thousand three hundred forty-six ten-thousandths_____

Write each number in standard form.

5. six hundred ninety-seven ten-thousandths _____0.0697_____

6. four thousand two hundred forty-six ten-thousandths _____0.4246_____

7. sixteen ten-thousandths _____0.0016_____

8. nine thousand nine hundred ninety-nine ten-thousandths _____0.9999_____

Name _____

Designing with Decimals

Shade in the decimal amount in each model.

1.

    0.2

2.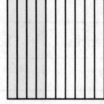

    0.4

3.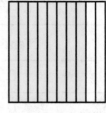

    0.8

4.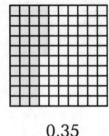

    0.35

5.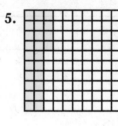

    0.24

6.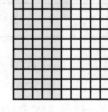

    0.52

Complete. You may look at your shaded models above.

7. 2 tenths = __20__ hundredths

8. __4__ tenths = 40 hundredths

9. 35 hundredths = __3__ tenths and 5 hundredths

10. 2 tenths and 4 hundredths = __24__ hundredths

Use colored pencils to make a design or picture on the grid.
Color the numbers of small squares needed to model the
decimals shown below. Check students' drawings.

Red = 0.25

Yellow = 0.30

Blue = 0.15

Black = 0.10

Green = 0.20

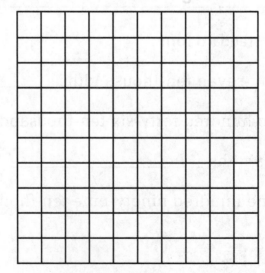

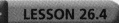

Missing Number Mystery

Write mixed numbers for the numbers that are missing from each number line below.

1.

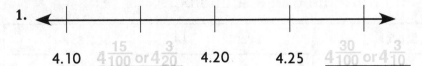

4.10 $4\frac{15}{100}$ or $4\frac{3}{20}$ 4.20   4.25 $4\frac{30}{100}$ or $4\frac{3}{10}$

2.

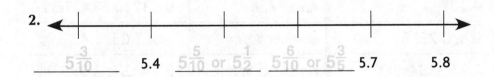

$5\frac{3}{10}$ 5.4 $5\frac{5}{10}$ or $5\frac{1}{2}$ $5\frac{6}{10}$ or $5\frac{3}{5}$ 5.7   5.8

3.

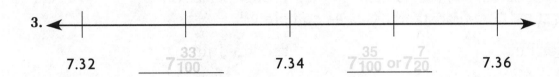

7.32 $7\frac{33}{100}$ 7.34 $7\frac{35}{100}$ or $7\frac{7}{20}$ 7.36

4.

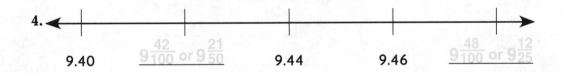

9.40 $9\frac{42}{100}$ or $9\frac{21}{50}$ 9.44   9.46 $9\frac{48}{100}$ or $9\frac{12}{25}$

5.

3.18   3.19 $3\frac{20}{100}$ or $3\frac{1}{5}$ 3.21 $3\frac{22}{100}$ or $3\frac{11}{50}$ 3.23

6.

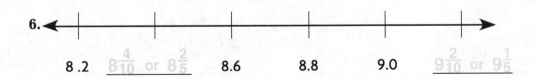

8 .2 $8\frac{4}{10}$ or $8\frac{2}{5}$ 8.6   8.8   9.0 $9\frac{2}{10}$ or $9\frac{1}{5}$

7. Make your own number line. Include the following numbers: 4.01, 4.12, 4.03, $4\frac{9}{100}$, $4\frac{2}{25}$, $4\frac{3}{20}$. Number lines may vary. A possible answer is shown.

4.01 4.02 4.03 4.04 4.05 4.06 4.07 $4\frac{2}{25}$ $4\frac{9}{100}$ 4.10 4.11 4.12 4.13 4.14 $4\frac{3}{20}$ 4.16 4.17

Name _____

First-Second-Third

At the recent Number Olympics, people were confused by who was in first, second, or third place. (HINT: *First* was always the least number and *third* the greatest number.)

Event	Scores	Event	Scores
Number Put	0.3, 0.4, 0.2	Fraction Jump	0.96, 1.53, 0.8
Decimal Hurdles	4.207, 4.281, 4.278	Area Swim	0.617, 0.674, 1.320
High Number	0.3, 0.28, 0.4	Number Beam	3.5, 3.05, 3.47
Freestyle Numbers	1.23, 0.84, 1.1	Perimeter Sprint	2.34, 2.4, 2.059

For each event listed, put the numbers in their proper places on the medals stand. The first stand has been completed.

Number Put

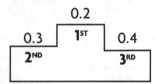

Fraction Jump

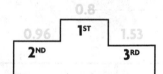

Decimal Hurdles

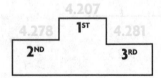

Area Swim

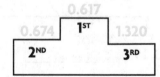

High Number

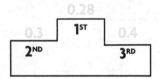

Number Beam

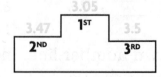

Freestyle Numbers

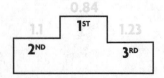

Perimeter Sprint

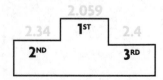

Name _____

Money Combos

Show three different coin combinations that equal each amount below. Use quarters, dimes, nickels, and pennies—at least one of each coin—in each combination.

Answers will vary.

1. $0.84

2 quarters, 2 dimes, 2 nickels, 4 pennies

2 quarters, 1 dime, 4 nickels, 4 pennies

1 quarter, 5 dimes, 1 nickel, 4 pennies

2. $0.55

1 quarter, 2 dimes, 1 nickel, 5 pennies

1 quarter, 1 dime, 3 nickels, 5 pennies

1 quarter, 1 dime, 1 nickel, 15 pennies

3. $1.37

4 quarters, 3 dimes, 1 nickel, 2 pennies

4 quarters, 2 dimes, 3 nickels, 2 pennies

3 quarters, 3 dimes, 6 nickels, 2 pennies

4. $2.46

9 quarters, 1 dime, 2 nickels, 1 penny

8 quarters, 3 dimes, 3 nickels, 1 penny

7 quarters, 5 dimes, 4 nickels, 1 penny

Name _____

Super (Market) Estimations

Cashiers can make errors, and scanners don't always scan the correct prices. It is important to check your receipt.

At the left is a list of your purchases. At the right is what the cash register rang up. Match the lists and circle the errors. By how much was the receipt off?

Purchases		Market Receipt
Facial tissues	$1.29	4.50
Fruit drink	$1.79	1.96
Rice	$1.69	0.65
Soap	$0.89	1.99
Apples—3 lbs. at	$1.50 lb.	2.98
Light bulbs	$2.89	0.97
Carrots	$0.65	1.29
Cereal	$3.49	3.49
Milk	$1.39	4.39
Butter	$1.99	8.90
Sugar	$0.79	1.56
Flour	$0.75	1.79
Soda	$3.49	0.30
Oatmeal	$1.56	1.39
Bagels	$3.00	0.75
Bread	$1.59	4.79
Mustard	$3.10	2.75
Cookies	$2.75	3.10
Chicken	$4.97	1.59

Total _____$42.57_____   **Total** _____$49.14_____

The receipt was off by _____$6.57_____.

CW144   Challenge

Name _____

Shop Till You Drop!

Estimate the cost of the items on each list. Circle the list that comes closer without going over your spending limit. Methods and estimates will vary. Rounded estimates are given.

1. Your spending limit is $400.

List 1		
Suit	$200	
Shirt	$40	
Shoes	$40	
Coat	$100	
Gloves	$10	

Suit	$185.40	Belt	$32.00
Shirt	$35.65	Coat	$115.40
Shoes	$43.75	Hat	$46.00
Tie	$27.65	Pants	$28.90
Gloves	$12.99	Suspenders	$34.81
Socks	$7.00		

List 2	
Coat	$100
Hat	$50
Shirt	$40
Suit	$200
Belt	$30

Estimated cost: ____$390____   Estimated cost: ____$420____

Actual cost: ____$393.19____   Actual cost: ____$414.45____

2. Your spending limit is $2,000.

List 1		
Computer	$1,200	
CD-ROM drive	$200	
Printer	$300	
Software	$200	
Speakers	$100	

Computer	$1,199.99	Joystick	$59.25
Laptop Computer	$1,499.95	Desk	$79.42
CD-ROM drive	$238.75	Speakers	$138.60
Printer	$318.66		
Software	$179.25		

List 2	
Laptop Computer	$1,500
Printer	$300
Software	$200

Estimated cost: ____$2,000____   Estimated cost: ____$2,000____

Actual cost: ____$2,075.25____   Actual cost: ____$1,997.86____

Play Ball

Place the numbers on the balls in the correct place in the diagram below so that the sum of these positions is the same: The sum b is always equal to 3.06.

- All of the outfield = b
- Catcher + Pitcher + Third Base + Left field = b
- Catcher + Pitcher + Shortstop + Center field = b
- Catcher + Pitcher + Second Base + Right field = b
- Catcher + Pitcher + First Base = b

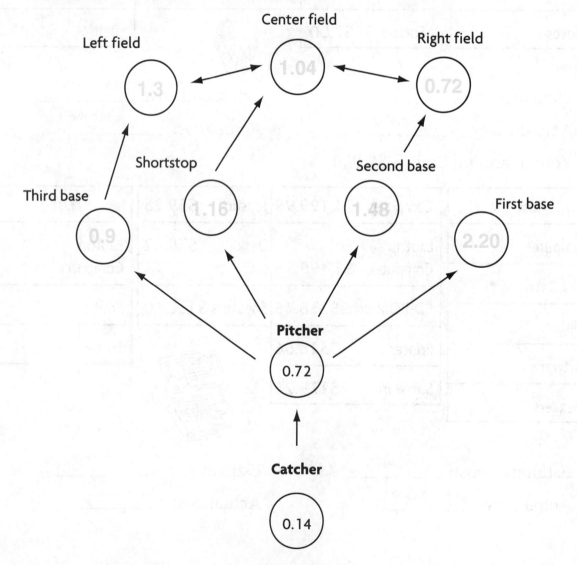

Amazing Mazes

Use number patterns to complete the empty boxes.

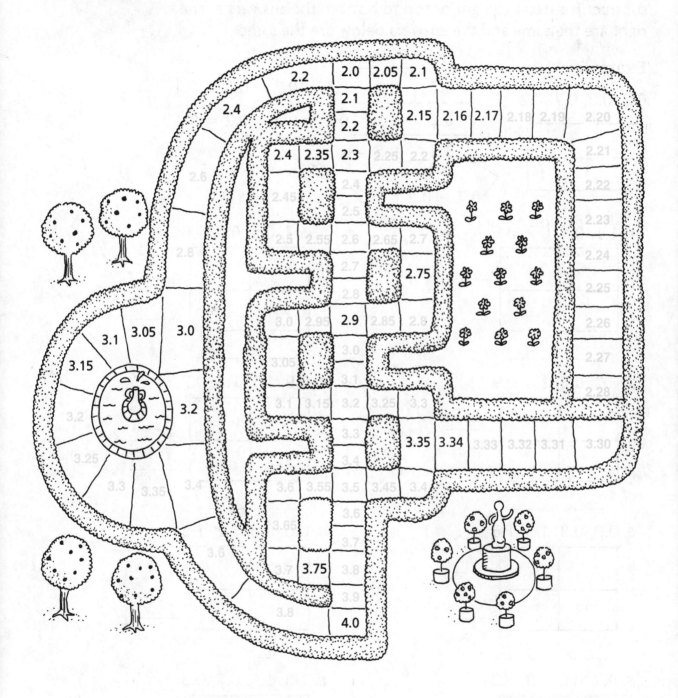

Addition and Subtraction Puzzles

Put the numbers in the boxes so that when you either add or
subtract from left to right or top to bottom the answers at the
right are the same and the answers below are the same.

Some answers may vary. Possible answers given.

Example:

0.2, 0.3, 0.7, 0.2

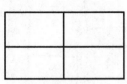

0.7	0.3	0.4	$0.7 - 0.3 = 0.4$
0.2	0.2	0.4	$0.2 + 0.2 = 0.4$

0.5   0.5

$0.3 + 0.2 = 0.5$

$0.7 - 0.2 = 0.5$

1. 1.1, 0.5, 0.2, 0.8

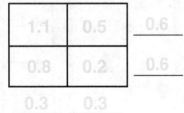

1.1	0.5	0.6
0.8	0.2	0.6

0.3   0.3

2. 1.7, 0.5, 0.6, 0.6

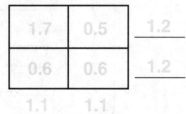

1.7	0.5	1.2
0.6	0.6	1.2

1.1   1.1

3. 0.2, 0.2, 1.3, 0.9

1.3	0.9	0.4
0.2	0.2	0.4

1.1   1.1

4. 0.9, 1.1, 1.3, 0.7

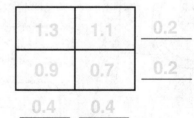

1.3	1.1	0.2
0.9	0.7	0.2

0.4   0.4

5. 0.9, 0.3, 1.2, 1.8

1.8	1.2	0.6
0.9	0.3	0.6

0.9   0.9

6. 0.6, 0.6, 1.2, 1.2

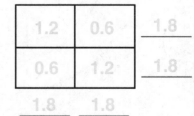

1.2	0.6	1.8
0.6	1.2	1.8

1.8   1.8

7. 0.2, 0.2, 0.3, 0.3

0.3	0.2	0.5
0.2	0.3	0.5

0.5   0.5

8. 1.3, 1.1, 0.7, 0.5

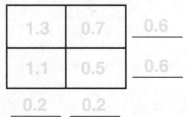

1.3	0.7	0.6
1.1	0.5	0.6

0.2   0.2

Think About It

The decimal point is missing from each of the numbers in Exercises 1–8.
Place the decimal point where it belongs in each number.

1. ___3 5___ number of seconds it takes Tony to write his name

2. ___1 7.7___ length of a new pencil in centimeters

3. ___1.7 7___ length of a bee in centimeters

4. ___2 0.3 6___ record speed in seconds for the 200-meter run

5. ___$ 1.2 5___ cost of a fancy helium-filled balloon

6. ___3.4 0___ number of miles walked in one hour

7. ___3 4.0___ number of miles driven in one hour

8. ___1 3 7.1___ height of an average fourth-grade student
   in centimeters

For 9–14, arrange the
digits shown to make the
described number.

9. Least number possible   _1_ _2_ . _3_ _4_

10. Greatest number possible   _5_ _4_ . _3_ _2_

11. Number nearest to 30   _3_ _1_ . _2_ _4_

12. Greatest number that is less than 35   _3_ _4_ . _5_ _2_

13. Least number that is greater than 20   _2_ _1_ . _3_ _4_

14. Number nearest to 10   _1_ _2_ . _3_ _4_

15. What would your answers to Exercises 9–14 be
    if the 5 card was replaced with a zero card?

01.23; 43.21; 30.12; 34.21; 20.13; 10.23

Not Always a Rectangle

On dot paper you can find the perimeter of a figure that is not a rectangle by counting the number of units around the figure.

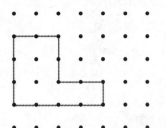
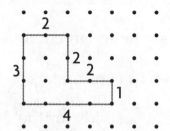

Starting along the left side, the figure is 3 units, 2 units, 2 units, 2 units, 1 unit, and 4 units.

So, the perimeter of the figure is:

3 units + 2 units + 2 units + 2 units + 1 unit + 4 units, or 14 units.

Find the perimeter of each figure.

1.

_____14 units_____

2.

_____16 units_____

3.
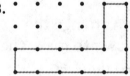

_____16 units_____

4.
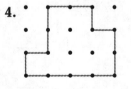

_____14 units_____

5.
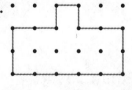

_____16 units_____

6.
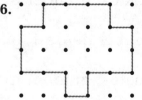

_____18 units_____

7.
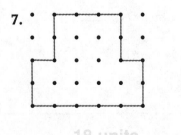

_____18 units_____

8.
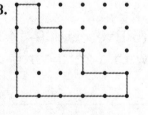

_____18 units_____

9.
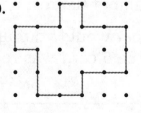

_____18 units_____

Block It Out!

Read the directions for making each figure. Draw, number, and color the figure on the grid below. Check students' drawings. Possible drawings shown.

1. Figure 1: Draw a square figure with a perimeter of 4, using 1 square. Color it red.

2. Figure 2: Draw a rectangular figure with a perimeter of 10, using 6 squares. Color it green.

3. Figure 3: Draw a square figure with a perimeter of 12, using 9 squares. Color it blue.

4. Figure 4: Draw a figure with a perimeter of 14, using 9 squares. Color it black.

5. Figure 5: Draw a figure with a perimeter of 12, using 5 squares. Color it yellow.

6. Figure 6: Draw a figure with a perimeter of 24, using 11 squares. Color it purple.

7. Figure 7: Draw a figure with a perimeter of 16, using 16 squares. Color it brown.

8. Figure 8: Draw a figure with a perimeter of 20, using 21 squares. Color it orange.

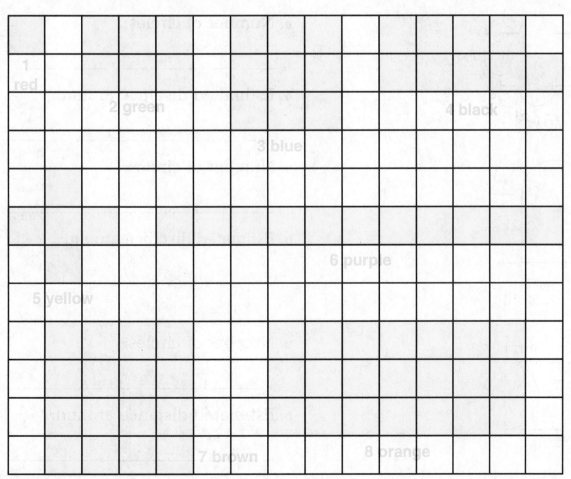

Circumference

Each figure below is made from parts of circles and rectangles. Tell how many circles are in the figure, and then estimate the distance around each figure.

1.

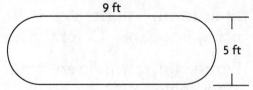

9 ft

5 ft

a. Number of circles:

_____one circle_____

b. Estimated distance around:

_____about 33 feet_____

2.

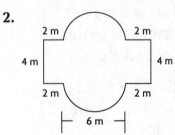

2 m 2 m
4 m 4 m
2 m 2 m
6 m

a. Number of circles:

_____one circle_____

b. Estimated distance around:

_____about 34 meters_____

3.

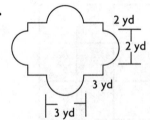

2 yd
2 yd
3 yd
3 yd

a. Number of circles:

_____two circles_____

b. Estimated distance around:

_____about 35 yards_____

4.

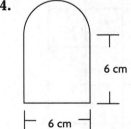

6 cm

6 cm

a. Number of circles:

_____half of a circle_____

b. Estimated distance around:

_____about 27 cm_____

5.

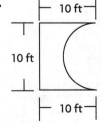

10 ft

10 ft

10 ft

a. Number of circles:

_____half of a circle_____

b. Estimated distance around:

_____about 45 feet_____

Formula Reasoning

You know the formula for the perimeter of a triangle is $P = a + b + c$. You also know perimeter formulas for other figures.

Perimeter of a rectangle: $P = 2 \times l + 2 \times w$, where l represents the length of the rectangle and w represents the width.

Perimeter of a square: $P = 4s$, where s represents the length of a side of the square.

Perimeter of a pentagon: $P = a + b + c + d + e$, where a, b, c, d, and e represent the lengths of the sides of the pentagon.

You can use the formula for the perimeter of a triangle to find the length of a missing side. You can also use the other perimeter formulas you know to find the length of a missing side of other figures.

Use a formula to solve.

1. A pentagon has a perimeter of 97 feet. The lengths of four of the sides are 18, 22, 17, and 21 feet. How long is the missing side?

    _____ 19 ft _____

2. A rectangular garden is 6 yards long. The perimeter of the garden is 18 yards. How wide is the garden?

    _____ 3 yd _____

3. A square window has a perimeter of 36 inches. How long is each side of the window?

    _____ 9 in. _____

4. A rectangle 30 inches wide has a perimeter of 160 inches. What is the length of the rectangle?

    _____ 50 in. _____

5. Four sides of a pentagon are each 15 centimeters. The perimeter of the pentagon is 80 centimeters. How long is the missing side?

    _____ 20 cm _____

6. Three sides of a pentagon are each 24 inches. The fourth side is 26 inches. The perimeter of the pentagon is 119 inches. How long is the missing side?

    _____ 21 in. _____

Name _____

Estimate Garden Areas

Maria draws diagrams of gardens for her friends. Each
garden contains a pond. Help Maria estimate the area of
each garden. Do not include the pond in your estimate.
Each square is 1 sq m. Possible estimates are given.

1.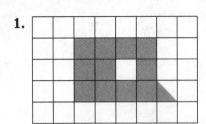

_____ 11.5 sq m _____

2.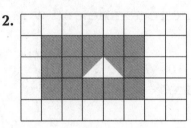

_____ 14 sq m _____

3.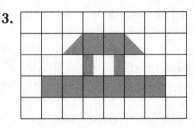

_____ 10 sq m _____

4.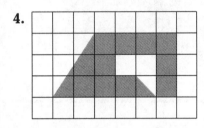

_____ 12 sq m _____

5.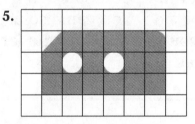

_____ 15.5 sq m _____

6.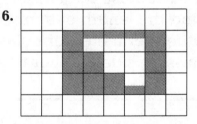

_____ 10.5 sq m _____

7.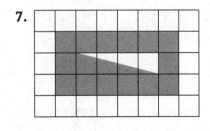

_____ 16 sq m _____

8.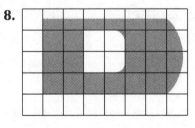

_____ 18.5 sq m _____

9.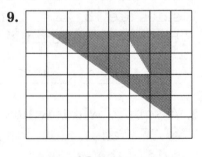

_____ 10 sq m _____

10.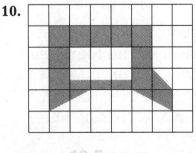

_____ 13.5 sq m _____

11.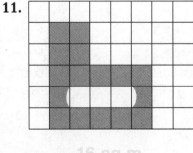

_____ 16 sq m _____

12.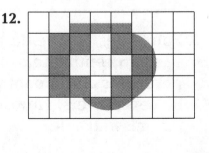

_____ 12 sq m _____

Unusual Measures

A very long time ago, people used body units to measure lengths.

Span — length from the end of the thumb to the end of the little finger when the hand is stretched fully

Cubit — length from the elbow to the longest finger

Fathom — length from fingertip to fingertip when arms are stretched fully in opposite directions

Pace — length of a walking step, measured from toe of back foot to toe of front foot

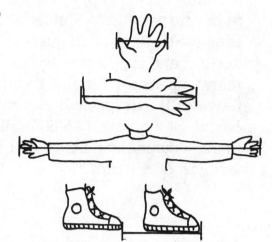

You can use body measures to find the perimeters and areas of objects at school. Record your results in the chart below. Answers will vary.

Object Measured	Measured in Spans		Measured in Cubits	
	Perimeter	Area	Perimeter	Area
Desk Top	14 spans	12 sq spans	9 cubits	$4\frac{1}{2}$ sq cubits
1.				
2.				
3.				
4.				

5. Measure the length and the width of your classroom in fathoms and in paces. Answers will vary.

length of classroom: _____ fathoms; _____ paces

width of classroom: _____ fathoms; _____ paces

Flying Carpet Ride

Solve.

1. Jasmine wrote a story about a flying carpet ride to Plume Island. She flew 4,638 miles north. Then she flew twice as many miles east. Finally, Jasmine flew south and reached Plume Island. She traveled 15,690 miles in all. How many miles was the last part of her trip?

_____ 1,776 mi _____

2. Jasmine's flying carpet not only flies—it also changes shape. The perimeter is always 32 feet. Jasmine needs the greatest area to take her new Plume Island friends for a ride. What polygon will give her the greatest possible area? What are the lengths of the sides?

_____ square; 8 ft × 8 ft _____

3. Two Islanders offered to buy Jasmine's carpet. Tirian offered her $500. Miraz offered her $7.50 per square foot. If the perimeter of the square carpet equals 32 feet, who offered more money? How much more?

_____ Tirian; $20 more than Miraz _____

4. Jasmine flew home by a more direct path. Her return flight was 5,555 miles shorter than her trip to Plume Island. How far was Jasmine's return flight? (Hint: See Problem 1.)

_____ 10,135 mi _____

5. Flying carpets give prizes if you travel more than 25,000 miles. Can Jasmine get a prize? How many miles did she fly? (Hint: See Problems 1 and 4.)

_____ yes; 25,825 mi _____

6. Write your own multistep problem about an adventure with a flying carpet. Show the solution upside down at the bottom of column 1.

_____ Check students' work. _____

_____

_____

_____

Answer:

Problem Solving Strategy

Find a Pattern

What if? Use the figures below to give examples that agree with
your answers to the "What If" question. Example numbers may vary.

1. **What if** the width of a rectangle
was doubled? What would
happen to the area of the
rectangle?

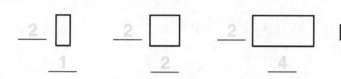

_____
The area is doubled.
_____

2. **What if** the width of a rectangle
was divided by 2? What would
happen to the area of the
rectangle?

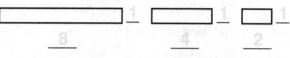

_____
The area is halved.
_____

3. **What if** the width of a rectangle
was tripled? What would happen
to the area of the rectangle?

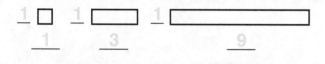

_____
The area is tripled.
_____

4. **What if** the width of a rectangle
was divided by 3? What would
happen to the area of the
rectangle?

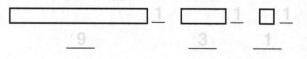

_____
The area is divided by 3.
_____

5. What do you think would happen to the area
of a rectangle whose width is multiplied by 4?
divided by 4?

_____
The area would be multiplied by 4; the area would be divided by 4.
_____

Riddle, Riddle

Name the plane or solid figure described by each riddle.

1. When you trace one surface of a cone or a cylinder, you see me. What am I?

   _____

   a circle

2. I have 6 flat faces that all look exactly the same. What am I?

   _____

   a cube

3. You see two sizes of me when you trace a rectangular prism. What am I?

   _____

   a rectangle

4. If you trace me six times, you make a cube. What figure am I?

   _____

   a square

5. I am a solid figure with one circular surface. What am I?

   _____

   a cone

6. If you trace my 5 faces, you will find a square and triangles. What am I?

   _____

   a square pyramid

7. I have 9 edges, 6 vertices, and 5 faces. What figure am I?

   _____

   triangular prism

8. I am a solid figure with no vertices or edges. What am I?

   _____

   a sphere

9. All 4 of my faces are identical. What solid figure am I?

   _____

   a triangular pyramid

Puzzle Watch

Here are two puzzles to solve.

1. A supermarket worker wants to know how many ways he can stack four cube-shaped boxes. He can stack them in 1, 2, 3, or 4 layers. Help by finding as many arrangements as you can. Draw the arrangements below. How many did you find?

_____ Some possible arrangements are shown. _____

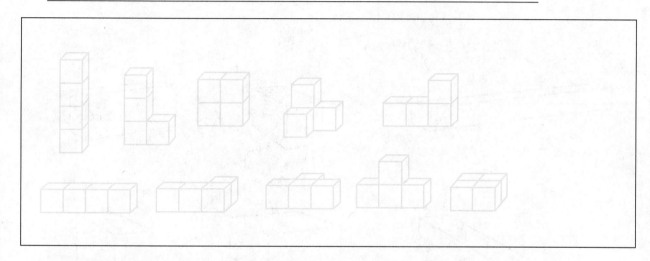

2. Use the five points shown below. Connect each point to *all* the other points. When you connect the five points, how many triangles can you find in the figure?
Drawings will vary. There are 35 triangles.

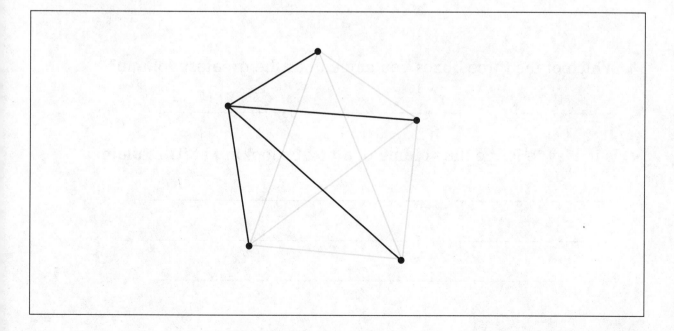

Estimate and Find Volume of Prisms

Circle the box in each row that has the greatest volume.

1.

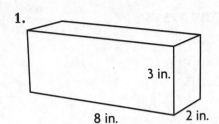 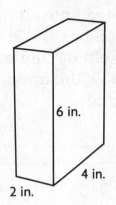 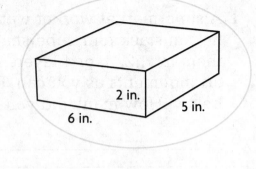

3 in.
8 in.   2 in.

6 in.
4 in.
2 in.

2 in.
6 in.   5 in.

2.

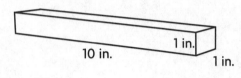 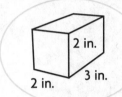 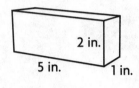

1 in.
10 in.
1 in.

2 in.
2 in.   3 in.

2 in.
5 in.   1 in.

3.

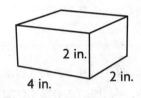   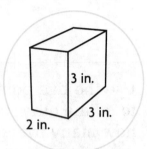

1 in.
8 in.
2 in.

2 in.
4 in.   2 in.

3 in.
2 in.   3 in.

4. Which of the three boxes you circled has the greatest volume?

The third box in Exercise 1 has the greatest volume.

5. Is it easy to judge the volume of a box by looking at it? Explain.

Accept any reasonable answer.

_____

_____

_____

Problem Solving Skill

Too Much/Too Little Information

Each of these problems has too little information. Supply each problem with reasonable data. Solve. Check students' work.

1. Marion wants to build a wooden box that is 20 centimeters long and 15 centimeters high. What is the volume of the box?

   Possible answer: The box is 10 cm wide; the volume

   of the box is 3,000 cubic cm.

2. Rebecca wants to build a box too. She wants it to have the same volume as Marion's, but a different width. Rebecca wants the box to be 20 centimeters long. What is the height and width of the box?

   Possible answer: The volume of the box is 3,000 cm;

   The box Rebecca builds can be 15 cm wide and

   10 cm high.

3. Michael bought some wood to build a box. He wants to build a box that is 10 inches long and 4 inches high. What is the volume of the box?

   Possible answer: The box is 10 in. wide; the volume

   of the box is 400 cubic in.